MW01030244

TRUE GRETCH

YOUNG ADULT EDITION

TRUE GRETCH

YOUNG ADULT EDITION

LESSONS FOR ANYONE WHO WANTS TO MAKE A DIFFERENCE

GRETCHEN WHITMER

with LISA DICKEY

atheneum

NEW YORK AMSTERDAM/ANTWERP
LONDON TORONTO SYDNEY NEW DELHI

$\mathcal{A}$
atheneum

An imprint of Simon & Schuster Children's Publishing Division
1230 Avenue of the Americas, New York, New York 10020
This work is a memoir. It reflects the author's present
recollections of her experiences over a period of years.
Copyright © 2024, 2025 by Super Deluxe, LLC
This young adult edition is adapted from *True Gretch* by Gretchen Whitmer,
published by Simon & Schuster in 2024
Jacket front panel photograph © 2012 by Anne C. Savage
All rights reserved, including the right of reproduction in whole or in part in any form.
Atheneum logo is a trademark of Simon & Schuster, LLC.
For information about special discounts for bulk purchases, please contact Simon & Schuster
Special Sales at 1-866-506-1949 or business@simonandschuster.com.
The Simon & Schuster Speakers Bureau can bring authors to your live event. For more
information or to book an event, contact the Simon & Schuster Speakers Bureau at
1-866-248-3049 or visit our website at www.simonspeakers.com.
The text for this book was set in Sabon LT.
Manufactured in the United States of America
First Edition
2 4 6 8 10 9 7 5 3 1
CIP data for this book is available from the Library of Congress.
ISBN 9781665983761
ISBN 9781665983785 (ebook)

Internet addresses and telephone numbers given in the book were accurate at the time it went to
press. The author and publisher are not responsible for changes to third-party websites.

For my daughters,
Sherry and Sydney

CONTENTS

TRUE GRETCH
YOUNG ADULT EDITION

PROLOGUE

When my siblings and I were little, our grandmother Esther Whitmer, whom we called Nino, gave us three pieces of advice: Work hard. Don't get married until you're at least twenty-eight. And never part your hair in the middle. Like any kid getting advice, I probably rolled my eyes. But as I got older, I saw that Nino was right about a few things.

My brother Richard, my sister Liz, and I all grew up to be very hard workers. When I was still in middle school, I mowed our lawn every week and babysat for neighborhood kids. As a teenager, I worked one summer as a cashier at Burlingame Lumber and another maintaining the buffet line (gross) at the Royal Fork Buffet. But my favorite job was at Target, because I worked with two of my best friends there. I still remember the day when one of them had to put price tags on boxes of condoms, and I could hear her cracking up from two aisles away.

As for Nino's other pieces of advice, none of us married before twenty-eight (although Liz barely made it, marrying right at that age). And I don't know what to tell you about that third one. Seriously, part your hair wherever you want. I don't happen to part mine in the middle, but it's totally fine if you do. What business is it of my grandmother's?

Nino, who was my dad's mom, didn't know everything, but she knew a lot. Born on a small farm in Ohio in 1913, she lived one hundred years, right through the whole roller-coaster ride of the twentieth century and well into the twenty-first. She lived to see two world wars, depressions and recessions, humans setting foot on the moon, and the dawn of the computer age. Nino used to tell us that the world had changed more in her century than during any other in history. She was probably right. And even if she wasn't, it's not cool to argue with your hundred-year-old grandmother.

My mom's side of the family had been in Michigan for generations. I loved growing up here. We used to take family trips to Lake Michigan, fishing, playing games, sitting around bonfires. During football season, my dad would take us to watch Michigan State games, and we'd bundle up in our MSU sweatshirts, snug against the autumn chill. In the winter, we'd go sledding and have snowball fights, and in warmer weather we'd gorge on the best cherries in the world. Michigan has a little bit of everything—all four seasons, the music of Motown, great classic cars from Detroit. I've lived here my whole life and never wanted to be anywhere else.

Our house was a small two-story white colonial in East Lansing, with a big corner-lot yard that had crabapple and birch trees. Dad built us a little tree house in the back, and we used it as a clubhouse—even though, as I think about it now, it probably wasn't particularly comfortable, or level, or even safe. The grown-ups had their own kind of clubhouse, a basement with a wet bar and red shag carpet, which every house seemed to have in the 1970s. But the best part of living in East Lansing was that we could walk to Spartan Stadium for the football games, or to MSU's Jenison Field House to see Magic Johnson play basketball. It's no surprise that I became a huge Spartan fan and would end up going to college there myself.

Nino and our grandfather Dana Whitmer, who we called Dano, lived in Pontiac, about an hour away by car. This meant I got to spend a lot of time with her, and we became close. Nino was an elementary school teacher, and she used to send me letters with math problems. I'd work through them, then mail my answers back. Though she wasn't able to turn me into a mathematician, I loved getting those letters, our special little tradition.

Nino set a great example for us. She was smart, strong, and funny, a rebel who wore white jeans year-round long before fashion icon Anna Wintour said that was okay. She drove until she was ninety-eight, and her last car was a cherry-red Oldsmobile convertible. (I'd be reluctant to give up driving too, with a car like that.) Her neighbors called her the "flower lady," because she put pink flowers in every window of her house and planted them in the park across the street. And she taught us that you can always find something good in a person. "Even the meanest person might have pretty eyes," she used to say. That advice stuck with me—the determination to always look for the good in any given person or situation.

So my grandmother had a big effect on me. I've tried to emulate her in many ways, and apparently that now includes offering advice. It's not that I think I'm the be-all-end-all or wiser than anyone else—far from it. I share the opinion of my dad, Dick Whitmer, who told a reporter during one of my early campaigns that "Gretchen knows she's not special." Thanks, Dad!

Actually, I knew what he meant—that I don't think I'm better than anyone else. He's the one who taught me that, after all, leading by example. Whenever we asked if we could bring friends along to fun events, like going to the Cedar Point amusement park, Dad would always say yes. He always made the point that not everyone had the same opportunities we did, so we should include people. "We're not special," he'd say. "We're just lucky."

So it's not that I think I have some kind of superior insight. But I have lived through some strange and difficult events, particularly in the past few years: Revealing on the floor of the Michigan Senate that I'd been sexually assaulted in college. Governing through pandemics, armed protests, and polar vortexes. Learning that certain members of a far-right militia planned to kidnap and assassinate me. It's hard to find the good in these situations, but following Nino's example, that's what I've tried to do. And I want to share what I've learned.

I feel honored to have served the people of Michigan for

more than twenty years, first as a state representative, then as a state senator, a prosecutor, and now as governor. And while my grandmother bore witness to most of the twentieth century, I've spent the first quarter of this century watching as the arc of our politics and the tone of public life has bent uncomfortably toward incivility and strife.

Traveling around the state and beyond, I often get the question "How do you stay positive in light of everything that's happening?" The world feels very heavy right now. War is raging in the Middle East and Ukraine. Xenophobia and hatred of "others" is on the rise. Young people are facing a whole range of fears, including the effects of climate change, gun violence, and worries about the job market. But we have to find a way to keep moving ahead, to embrace our community and love our neighbors. We have to figure out how to do the next right thing, whatever that may be. And yes, the phrase "do the next right thing" is from a song in *Frozen II*, but the sentiment is real, and it's one we desperately need these days.

That's why I decided to write this book: to put a little light out there in a dark time. If I can tell a story that will help you feel less alone, or share something I wish I'd known when I was younger, or even make you laugh—that's what it's all about.

So, settle in, or if you feel like it, take some time to make a pan of Nino's famous clover rolls to snack on while you read. The recipe, from a family cookbook my sister made called *Cooking with Halfwhits*, is on the next page.

Nino's Clover Rolls

Ingredients

1 cup warm water
1 pkg dry yeast (2 1/4 teaspoons)
1/4 cup sugar
3 1/2 cups flour
6 T butter chopped into small pieces (salted okay)
1 egg
1 heaping teaspoon table salt

Directions

Note: By hand or mixer with a dough hook it's important to add ingredients in the order they are listed: water, yeast, sugar, flour, butter, egg, salt. (Yeast likes sugar but salt will kill it, so keep them apart before mixing.)

Mix with a wooden spoon or in mixer first with paddle attachment then when mostly incorporated, switch to dough hook. Mix with dough hook on low for about 6-8 minutes. Alternatively, mix with spoon until ingredients come together then knead by hand. Dough should be smooth and not very sticky.

Put dough in oiled bowl and cover with plastic wrap. Set in warm place for 90 minutes or until it has doubled in size. Spray a 12 cup muffin pan with nonstick spray. Divide dough into 12 equal pieces and then divide those into 3 pieces. Roll them into balls and place them in each prepared cup. Let rise again covered in a warm spot for around 75 minutes. When they look puffy, bake in a 350 degree oven for 15-18 minutes. Turn halfway if it is getting too brown on one side.

```
Dinner Rolls                    Esther

  1 pkg dry yeast
  1 c warm water
  6 T shortning-Crisco
  1 t salt
  ¼ c sygar

  Put yeast in cup,¼½ pour on 2 T water
  Put the shortning, sugar, salt in remaining H₂0
  Add 1 egg
  Add yeast mixture
  Stir in 3½ c flour gradually (-put in regrig now
  Let rise 1½ hours, till double in size
  bake 10-12 min at 425 in top part of oven
```

CHAPTER 1

DON'T LET THE BULLIES GET YOU DOWN

In 1981, when I was ten years old, the TV show *Three's Company* was a huge hit. It was a silly comedy about two women and a man sharing an apartment, a situation that back then was seen as a little bit shocking. Everybody in my fifth-grade class watched it, tuning in every Tuesday night to see what kind of trouble Jack, Janet, and Chrissy were getting into.

In November of that year, the show introduced a new character named Greedy Gretchen. Played by actress Teresa Ganzel, Greedy Gretchen was a blond bombshell who wore a spaghetti-strap dress to show off her ample bosom. Unfortunately for me, I had started developing earlier than other girls in my class, so even in the fifth grade, I was already getting kind of busty. Not surprisingly, some of the boys started calling me Greedy Gretchen. Did I hate it? You bet I did. The only thing worse than having boobs suddenly sprout on your fifth-grade body is having hormonal boys point it out every three minutes. At age ten, I really didn't want to stand out. But what could I do about it?

I hated that nickname, but I didn't know how to respond. When I was a kid, people used to say, "Just ignore it." Or worse: "If a boy teases you, it means he likes you." No one ever suggested that I stand up for myself, and so I didn't. The boys kept calling me Greedy Gretchen until middle school, when most of the other girls finally started developing too.

If I could go back and talk to my ten-year-old self, I'd tell her to share with a trusted adult what was going on. Ask for help. Advocate for herself. And I'll be honest: I still struggle with doing this sometimes. Because even as adults, women get unwanted commentary on how we look (more on this later). People sometimes judge us more on what we're wearing, rather than our intellect, our humor, our empathy. When that happens, it's okay to tell them that what they're doing isn't right. And if you see that a friend is going through it, it's okay to step up and support them, too. Add your voice to encourage people to focus on what matters.

Greedy Gretchen was just the first of many nicknames. A few years later, I went to a summer church camp in West Virginia. Our family wasn't super religious, but my parents divorced when I was six, and my mom and stepfather used to take us to Cascade Christian Church on the weekends we were with her. For whatever reason, the youth group took an annual trip all the way to West Virginia, so that's where I was the summer after I got my braces off.

I used to love these trips, because we'd all pile into a bus and just cut up and laugh all the way through the eight-hour ride. Dad used to joke that we packed enough food for two weeks just for the bus trip. Some of my best friends were in this church group, and it was exciting to take a trip together, away from our parents, to run wild at this camp five hundred miles from home.

One afternoon, we were playing a game that involved running all over the place, and another girl went to tag me. But instead of just tagging, she pushed the hell out of me (so much for church camp), and I went flying face-first into the cement. The impact knocked out both of my front teeth, scraped up my hands, and opened a huge gash on my knee. We were out in the woods, in the middle of nowhere, and with blood gushing out of my knee, the counselors had to improvise, using maxi pads to clean it up. When I finally got to the hospital, it took thirty stitches to close the cut, and the doctors sent me home tooth-less and in a wheelchair.

I looked awful, but I wasn't worried about what my friends might think. I mostly dreaded seeing my dad. He'd just paid thousands of dollars for braces to fix the gap between my front teeth—and now they were gone. All that money, wasted! I was so worried he would be mad that I was actually glad to have been hurt so badly, because he might feel sorry for me instead.

When I got back to Michigan with my busted face and torn-up knee, my dad could only shake his head. Gravity Gretchen, he called me, and the nickname stuck. I had always been a klutzy child, banging into things and falling, and even though that girl had pushed me, this episode served to cement my reputation. But unlike when the boys nicknamed me Greedy Gretchen, I didn't mind Gravity Gretchen. It was funny because it was true. And because my dad laughed when he called me that, it helped me learn how not to take myself too seriously.

People gave me other nicknames over the years: Stretchin' Gretchen, Fetchin' Gretchen, and much later, Big Gretch. But there was one nickname in particular that managed to propel me into the newspapers—though, in fairness, the coverage came about not so much because of the nickname itself, but because of who gave it to me.

"That woman from Michigan." That's me! President Donald J. Trump bestowed this very special name on me in the spring of 2020—though what he actually said, speaking to Vice President Mike Pence at a White House press conference, was "Don't call the woman in Michigan." It was his latest salvo in a battle that had been brewing between us for weeks, ever since Covid-19 began shutting down the country and growing numbers of Michiganders were dying.

In the early days of the pandemic, the White House didn't take it seriously enough. As hospitals overflowed and makeshift morgues filled up, governors scrambled to get basic medical supplies such as masks, surgical gloves, and ventilators. Detroit was hit particularly hard, along with New York City, Chicago, and New Orleans. We hoped and expected that the federal government would help, but instead, the president pitted the states against each other in a cruel *Hunger Games*–style scramble for equipment.

After I pointed out the lack of a federal strategy to combat Covid during a March 16 interview on MSNBC, Trump took to Twitter—now called X—the next morning to chastise me. "Failing Michigan Governor must work harder and be much more proactive. We are pushing her to get the job done. I stand with Michigan!" he tweeted at 9:27 a.m. Well, good morning! So I tweeted right back: "Now that I've got your attention, Mr. President—attack tweets won't solve this crisis. But swift and clear guidance, tests, personal protective equipment, and resources would."

I didn't love that the president of the United States was calling me out, but that was a very minor concern compared to what really mattered. Getting help for people was my job. That's what was important. If I'd lost the plot, or begun to think that this was all about me, I might have gotten distracted. But leadership isn't about protecting your own ego, it's about keeping your eye on the ball. So I stayed focused on trying to get the supplies we needed to keep people alive in Michigan.

At that time, in late March of 2020, the whole world had turned upside down. I had planned to have an eighteenth birthday party for my daughter Sherry, but instead, her school—and every other school in Michigan—was shut down during her senior year. As a parent, I was heartbroken for my kids. As a governor, my focus had to be protecting the people of Michigan.

When the districts shut down our schools, we had no idea how long that might last. No one had lived through anything like this before. (To find out how my daughters Sherry and Sydney felt about this, and many other events described in this book, check out the Q&A with them in the back.)

On Thursday, March 26, I requested that the Federal Emergency Management Agency (FEMA) declare a federal disaster in Michigan, which would release funds for our state. At least seven other states had already received this designation, and I wanted to make sure Michiganders got the federal dollars we needed. Trump didn't like it. His ego was bruised, because he takes things personally. He makes everything about himself, rather than about helping others.

He called in to the conservative commentator Sean Hannity's show that evening, and amid a rambling forty-minute interview, he said, "And your governor of Michigan, I mean, she's not stepping up. I don't know if she knows what's going on. But all she does is sit there and blame the federal government. She doesn't get it done." He took a moment to complain about Washington governor Jay Inslee, then came back to me, saying, "We've had a big problem with the young, a woman governor from, you know who I'm talking about, from Michigan." Did he not know my name? Or was he just acting like he was too far above me to speak it?

I decided to help him out. "Hi, my name is Gretchen Whitmer, and that governor is me," I tweeted, shortly after the Hannity interview aired. "I've asked repeatedly and respectfully for help. We need it. No more political attacks, just PPEs, ventilators, N95 masks, test kits. You said you stand with Michigan—prove it." I had been governor for only a little over a year, and getting into a fight with the president wasn't something I was keen to do. I did it because I was scared. Michiganders were dying, and I had to do whatever it took to get the federal government's attention and help. The great South African leader Nelson Mandela once wrote that courage is not the absence of fear, but the triumph over it. I had to face down my fear in order to keep Michiganders safe.

The next day, March 27, was the day Trump talked about me at the White House news briefing. Once again complaining about how governors were too demanding and not "appreciative" enough, he relayed advice that he'd supposedly given to Vice President Pence. "I say, 'Mike, don't call the governor of Washington. You're wasting your time with him. Don't call the woman in Michigan.' . . . You know what I say? If they don't treat you right, I don't call."

And then it was off to the races for That Woman from Michigan. People jumped at the chance to tweet about it, talk about it, even make T-shirts and bumper stickers with it. My team sent out emails quoting the nickname, instantly turning it from a liability into an advantage. One woman even got an image of my face and the words "That woman" tattooed on her leg. And when another sent me a blue T-shirt with the phrase

stenciled in giant white letters, I wore it during a video interview on *The Daily Show* with Trevor Noah.

To this day, people are still selling That Woman from Michigan
stickers, mugs, shirts, candles (scented with "lime, rose, geranium,
& musk"), pillows, trucker hats, and even nail polish (handmade,
toxin- and cruelty-free, in Traverse City). So, it was not only good
for me; you could argue that it's been good for Michigan's Etsy
community. And it only happened because I refused to let the president define me. I took his insult, flipped it, and made it my own.

That's the secret to dealing with bullies: You take their
weapon and make it your shield. You can't let their words get
to you or take them to heart. Knowing that you are worthy of
respect, from others but also from yourself, is an important
step in developing a strong sense of self.

Every time Trump gave me a nickname, I made it my own. On March 27, 2020, he tweeted, "I love Michigan, one of the reasons we are doing such a GREAT job for them during this horrible Pandemic. Yet your Governor, Gretchen 'Half' Whitmer is way in over her head, she doesn't have a clue. Likes blaming everyone for her own ineptitude!" Oooh, "half-Whit." Good one! Good enough to put on the cover of our family cookbook, where it makes me laugh every time I see it. (Liz and I now call our kids half-Whits too, since they're half Whitmer.) And hey—at least the president finally learned my name.

Our family cookbook

• • • •

Sometimes bullies need a taste of their own medicine. In late 2011, when I was in the Michigan State Senate, the Republican majority passed a supposedly anti-bullying bill. They named it Matt's Safe School Law, after a fourteen-year-old student named Matt Epling who took his life after upperclassmen hazed and assaulted him. Matt, who had lived in my district, was an honor roll student and a sweet kid whose fellow eighth graders voted him "Best Smile" and "Best Personality." His suicide was shocking and tragic, and it would have been entirely appropriate to honor his memory by naming a true anti-bullying bill after him.

But at the last minute, the Catholic Church, among others, pressured the bill's authors into adding language exempting people who bully for a "sincerely held religious belief or moral conviction." Seriously? This made a complete mockery of what the bill was supposed to do, giving anyone a free pass to bully if they claimed to be religious. Matt's dad, Kevin Epling, said it "tarnished the memory" of his son. In a floor speech, I tore into the stupidity of it, saying, "Not only does this not protect kids who are bullied, it further endangers them by legitimizing excuses for tormenting a student. After the way you've gutted it, it wouldn't have done a damn thing to save Matt! This is worse than doing nothing! It's a Republican license to bully."

That phrase gave my team an idea. We printed up a big cartoon of Senate majority leader Randy Richardville, showing him holding a driver's license with the words "License to Bully."

Now, I didn't have any personal beef with Randy, and in fact we were good friends. He and I served together for many years in the House and the Senate. The world is small in some ways, and it's smart to build relationships—even with people who have different beliefs than you do, because you'll probably cross paths again somewhere down the road. Getting to know one another takes energy and effort, but it helps you find common ground. And whatever differences we might have politically, in the end we're all people.

So, Randy and I have known and liked each other for years. But creating that cartoon seemed like the best way to draw attention to the sheer callousness of the bill they were trying to push through. It distilled the argument, making it very easy for the public to see the impact of bullying. And while Randy wasn't thrilled about seeing his caricature up in front of the Senate, he respected the creativity. Because here's the thing: it worked. The Republicans changed tack, adopting the House version of the bill, which condemned bullying full stop—no exemptions.

Politics can feel like a blood sport these days. Luckily for me, we Whitmers have thick skin and short memories. We each learned early on that by turning insults into humor and laughing at ourselves, we can take away their sting. That's why, on my high school powder puff football jersey, I chose the name Greedy. It's why Liz wears a necklace that says "Elizabitch." And it's why Richard wears a big old belt buckle with the name DICK on it. You can't make fun of us, because we're going to beat you to it. It's the best way to disarm bullies, by turning their weapon into your shield. You can trust me on this, or I'm not That Woman from Michigan.

A NOTE ON GALLOWS HUMOR

If you've read this far, you know how much I love humor. But what the Whitmers really love is gallows humor. The darker the better.

Once, when Richard was little, he was mouthing off to my mom while they were driving in Grand Rapids. She got fed up, pulled the car over, yanked him out, and gave him a spanking right by the side of the road (a more commonplace punishment in those days, though it was still pretty rare for our parents to spank us). By chance, she happened to have pulled the car over at a funeral home—and to this day, every time my sister or I drive past that funeral home, we snap a picture with our cell phones and text it to him. No comment, no text, just the picture.

After some in a right-wing militia plotted to kidnap and kill me in 2020—a shocking turn of events that you'll read about in a later chapter—I would talk about it on the campaign trail. "What doesn't kill you makes you stronger. So I guess I'm strong as hell now!" At the 2022 state Democratic convention,

I decided my walkout song should be "I'm Still Standing," by Elton John.

My favorite dark-humor moments, though, have been with my friend Rich Brown, who served as a state representative and is now the clerk of the Michigan House. Rich is hilarious, a longtime fixture in state politics who always has a smile for everyone. He's a big guy, tall and burly, but the most noticeable thing about him is that in place of his left arm, which he lost in a lawnmower accident as a child, he's got a prosthetic hook. When we were serving together in the House, I'd say, "Well, I'm the chairperson, but Rich is my number two. He's my right-hand man!" And people would look utterly aghast, like, *What in the hell is wrong with this woman?* Then Rich would say, "Yeah, and don't piss me off, because I've got a mean left hook!"

My mom, Sherry Whitmer, was the queen of finding something funny even in the darkest of times, and she passed that skill along to Richard, Liz, and me.

A little background on my siblings: in any family of three, alliances are always shifting. There were times we didn't get along or were mad at each other, but as adults, we've come to appreciate the depth of our relationships. We know all the stupid family stories. We're the only ones who can roast our parents and remember the silly stuff from our childhoods. We can finish each other's sentences. We'd crush the competition in any board game. Our family bond is strong.

Now, a little background on my mom: she was a hardworking

and successful lawyer, an assistant attorney general in Michigan who wore her accomplishments lightly and never took herself too seriously. Her laugh was infectious and so loud it once got us kicked out of a restaurant.

Though we always loved each other, we clashed hard when I was a teenager. I felt like I could do nothing right and that she was mad at me all the time. It seemed to me that Liz was her favorite child—and she probably was. My mom was hard on me because I was lazy in school and just wanted to have fun with my friends. I was a bit of a hellion, drinking and getting suspended from school, and when she was angry with me, she would yell. Sometimes I would yell back. So these were tough years in our relationship.

Moving, as well as having a new stepfather and stepbrother who came with a very flatulent dog, was a lot of change for my ten-year-old self, and I struggled for a bit, which might be why I became a troublemaker, so we clashed hard in those years.

After I left home for college, though, my mom and I were able to appreciate each other more. As I moved into adulthood, we became very close.

In 2000, she was diagnosed with glioblastoma multiforme—the same kind of deadly brain tumor that later took the life of John McCain and Beau Biden. After her first surgery, we hugged and cried, and then I climbed onto the hospital bed next to her. It was the most terrifying, heartbreaking, wrenching time I can remember.

As we lay there together, she said, "Well, Gretchen, at least I know you'll be the best senator there ever was." Then she paused. "Or, wait—you're running for the House." And we both just cracked up. It was hilariously funny, and we ended up laughing so hard we could hardly breathe. Her husband (my stepfather) walked in, expecting to find us weeping, and looked at us like, *What the hell?*

When the doctors told her she had only four to six months to live, she was scared.* But somehow, she still found ways to laugh. One of her favorite dark jokes was inspired by the 1990 movie *Kindergarten Cop*. Arnold Schwarzenegger plays a police detective who goes undercover as a kindergarten teacher. At one point, he puts his head in his hands and complains of a headache, and a little boy suggests he might have a tumor. "It's NAHT a TUMAAA," Arnold barks back in his thick Austrian accent, and we all found that so funny, we used to say it whenever one of us had a headache. When Mom got sick, she took to saying, "It's NAHT a TUMAAA! Oh wait—it actually is!"

It's so important to be able to find the light, even if the light is a dumb, filthy, or totally inappropriate joke. I still laugh when I think of that moment with my mom. It beats remembering the really sad moments, which we'll all have many of in our lives.

---

* In typical fashion, my mother thoroughly outperformed, living another eighteen months.

Baby Liz and me with our beautiful mom, 1973

CHAPTER 2

NEVER GIVE UP

I love listening to music, but there's one song that I can't bear to hear. Sinéad O'Connor's "Nothing Compares 2 U" is hauntingly beautiful. It was a huge hit in 1990, playing on the radio constantly when I was a freshman at Michigan State University. And that's why I can't stand hearing it. Because it takes me right back to the traumatic event that happened to me that year, when I was raped by another student.

At first, I didn't tell anyone. Not my friends, my siblings, my parents—no one. I felt ashamed, even though I hadn't done anything wrong. It's normal to question yourself, but I wish I'd known then that just because it happened didn't mean I deserved it, and it didn't mean it was my fault. No combination of decisions one person makes ever justifies another person's bad acts. Which meant that I was not responsible for what someone else did to me.

At the time, though, the assault rocked my sense of the world and my place in it. And I was terrified that I might be pregnant with my attacker's baby. To my immense relief, I wasn't. But if I had been, I at least knew that the choice of how to handle that situation would have been entirely up to me.

The ability to make decisions about your body and your future should be yours alone. Unfortunately, that's not the case right now for many Americans. As I write this, about a third of women in this country live in states where they have no right or access to abortion care. Women and girls are forced to risk their lives to see through an unwanted pregnancy. Some are told they must give birth to their attackers' children, even if the attacker is a father or stepfather or brother. In some states, the rapist can sue for parental rights. Just think about that for a moment, and what it really means. It's bad enough when any woman is raped. Taking away her right to determine what happens next with her body is inhumane.

Over the years, I revealed the assault only to a handful of partners, including my first husband, Gary Shrewsbury, and the man I married in 2011, Marc Mallory. Other than that, I didn't talk about it, and I tried hard not to think about it. My feeling was that bad things happen to people all the time. Better not to dwell on them, but instead just forge ahead as best we can.

As I look back now, I realize that I didn't know where to go to seek help dealing with the trauma. We knew that sexual assaults happened, but no one really talked about how to report them and how to deal with the aftermath. Now these conversations are much more in the open, and the public has gotten more educated. In the back of this book, there are resources for survivors of sexual assault, as well as resources for other struggles your or your friends might be facing.

Fast-forward more than two decades. In 2013, I was serving as Michigan's Senate minority leader, in a government dominated by Republicans from the governor's office through the House and Senate. That year, the Republicans tried to push through a bill requiring women in Michigan to buy extra health insurance for abortion coverage—even in cases of rape or incest. If you got pregnant from an assault and hadn't pre-bought the insurance, well, too bad. You couldn't buy it after getting pregnant, regardless of the circumstances.

This was not only cruel, it was absurd. Did lawmakers really expect women to "plan ahead" for a potential pregnancy resulting from a possible future assault? Passing this law was essentially requiring women to buy rape insurance. It was infuriating.

Polls showed that Michigan voters opposed it too, and Republican governor Rick Snyder had vetoed similar legislation a year prior. But the anti-abortion group Right to Life sidestepped the opposition by gathering enough signatures on a petition to bring the measure directly to the legislature. If the House and Senate passed this bill, the governor couldn't veto it this time, because it was a citizens' petition. This was a terrible loophole in the law, an end run on women's rights. And the Republicans, knowing there was strong opposition to the bill, decided not to hold any hearings on it, to stifle any dissent. They just wanted to get the thing passed.

The Republicans knew what they were doing was not popular. But they did it anyway. By refusing to have hearings, they wouldn't have to listen to women explain how devastating these laws would be. There were only two women in the Republican caucus at that point, so without hearings, it was obvious that women's voices wouldn't be widely heard. Our country was founded on the idea of individual freedoms, and this bill would curtail them, without even giving the people whom it would affect most a voice in the matter.

In fact, those of us who opposed the bill would have only one chance to speak against it, on the day it came up for a vote. My staff and I prepared a speech for me to give on the Senate floor, whenever that day came. I was angry, and the prepared remarks reflected that. They were personal and emotional, but they did not include the fact that I had been raped. Because no one on my staff had any idea that had happened.

In the Michigan Senate, a bill gets read into the record three times before a vote is taken. The first time, the secretary of the Senate just announces its title—basically a heads-up that it's coming. The second time, the secretary announces that the bill is open for debate. If you want to reserve time to speak for or against it, you push a button on your Senate desk, which registers your name on an electronic board. Staffers can't push that button—it has to be you. So, if you've popped out to go to the bathroom, or you miss the announcement, or you just don't get to your desk fast enough, the majority party can "call the question," cutting off debate before you get your chance to speak. (When the majority is abusing power, this is a move they regularly deploy.) The third time is when senators get up to speak.

On December 11, 2013—a date I'll never forget, because it happened to be Nino's one hundredth birthday—the secretary announced the Abortion Insurance Opt-Out Act. Today was the day, our one chance to try to persuade the Republican side how cruel and unfair this bill really was. Not only would it penalize women who became pregnant through assault, it would also affect women who had miscarriages and needed a procedure called dilation and curettage (D&C) to remove fetal tissue.

I knew that my Democratic colleague Jim Ananich and his wife Andrea had been trying to have a baby, and that they had, sadly, suffered a recent miscarriage. He and I had already talked about how this law would affect them, since their insurance would no longer cover all the necessary medical treatment upon any future pregnancy loss. Don't get me wrong; I believe that women should have access to abortions and be in complete control of what happens to our own bodies, no matter whether we're trying to get pregnant or not. But I thought that Jim and Andrea's story, involving a couple who desperately wanted children yet would still be penalized by this law, might resonate with the other side.

After the secretary announced the bill for the first time, I walked to Jim's desk, knelt beside him, and quietly asked if he would be willing to speak on the floor about how the law would affect his family. But the miscarriage had happened very recently, and the pain was just too raw. "I'm sorry," he told me, his face drawn and tense. "I just can't talk about it."* I told him I understood and then got up to walk back to my desk.

And that's when it hit me. Yes, Jim had a personal story that might make a difference if he shared it that day. But so did I. How could I ask him to publicly bare his soul if I wasn't willing to do that myself?

The secretary read the bill into the record for the second time, and I quickly pushed the button on my desk. My name popped up on the board behind a few Republicans who'd already been slotted in—a common tactic by the party in power, putting their people first so they can front-load the narrative. Knowing I had a short window before my turn to speak, I grabbed my executive assistant, Nancy Bohnet, and communications director, Bob McCann, and pulled them into the caucus room.

With so little time, I had to get right to the point. I told them I had been raped in college and that I was considering talking about it in my floor speech. Then I asked what they thought.

Nancy immediately said, "Don't do it. It won't change any votes, and you'll be making yourself vulnerable." Nancy, who had been with me for my whole political career—and is with

---

* Jim has since spoken publicly about it, and he and Andrea gave me permission to tell this story.

me to this day—is a strong and politically savvy woman. She knew the Republicans would vote party line, no matter what I said in my speech. Beyond that, she genuinely cared about how this revelation might affect me. She was looking out for me.

I turned to Bob, whose face was pale. "I don't have any advice," he said. "I can't even put myself in your place. You should do whatever you think is right."

We headed back into the chamber, and soon enough, it was my turn to speak. I walked up to the lectern, my prepared speech in hand, still unsure what to do.

"Thank you, madam chair," I said. "I rise for my 'no' vote explanation." Then I began reading my remarks:

> I rise in opposition to the so-called citizens' initiative before us that would require Michigan women to pay for a separate insurance rider to cover abortions, regardless of the circumstances surrounding their pregnancy.
>
> Apparently, the holiday season of goodwill toward men reads more like your will toward women, as the Republican male majority continues to ignorantly and unnecessarily weigh in on important women's health issues that they know nothing about.
>
> As a legislator, a lawyer, a woman, and the mother of two girls, I think the fact that

rape insurance is even being discussed by this body is repulsive, let alone the way it has been orchestrated and shoved through this legislature.

And for those of you who want to act aghast that I'd use a term like "rape insurance" to describe the proposal here in front of us, you should be even more offended that it's [an] absolutely accurate description of what this proposal requires. This tells women who were raped and became pregnant that they should have thought ahead and bought special insurance for it. . . .

I've said it before and I will say it again. This is by far one of the most misogynistic proposals I've ever seen in the Michigan legislature.

I delivered my remarks as deliberately and forcefully as possible, letting my anger show. In the back of my mind, though, my thoughts were spinning. For twenty-three years, I had pushed down the awful memory of what happened to me in college. I never in my life imagined talking about it in a public forum. Yet suddenly, in the course of one short speech, with TV cameras rolling, I had to decide whether to reveal my deepest secret to the world. Once it was out, there would be no turning back.

My mouth went dry. It was terrifying to think of opening myself up, of telling this room full of mostly men about being assaulted as a young woman. (At that time, there were more men named John than total women in the Senate, five to four.) I was just in turmoil. But the longer I spoke, the more I realized I had to do it.

They weren't really listening to me, because what I was saying was too abstract. And the only way to cut through the noise was by revealing my own story. Personal stories are powerful, and telling mine felt like the only way to make these legislators understand that this law would harm real people.

So, with only a few minutes left of my time, I put my papers aside and began speaking off-the-cuff. "I have a lot more prepared remarks here," I said, "but I think it's important for me to just mention a couple of things."

I spoke briefly about a woman named Jenny Lane, who had written a letter opposing the bill. I mentioned having "a colleague" whose wife's pregnancy went awry and required a D&C, taking care not to name him. Finally, I gathered my courage and began speaking the words that I had never imagined saying in public.

> I'm about to tell you something that I have not
> shared with many people in my life. But over
> twenty years ago, I was a victim of rape. And
> thank God it didn't result in a pregnancy, because
> I can't imagine going through what I went through
> and then having to consider what to do about an
> unwanted pregnancy from an attacker. And as a

mother with two girls, the thought that they would ever go through something like I did keeps me up at night.

At the mention of my daughters, my voice broke. I was fighting back tears, but after taking a moment to compose myself, I went on.

I thought this was all behind me. You know how tough I can be. The thought and the memory of that still haunts me. If this were law then, and I had become pregnant, I would not be able to have coverage, because of this. How extreme—how extreme does this measure need to be?

I am not the only woman in our state that has faced that horrible circumstance. I am not enjoying talking about it. It's something I've hidden for a long time. But I think you need to see the face of the women that you are impacting by this vote today. I think you need to think of the girls that we're raising and what kind of a state we want to be, where you would put your approval on something this extreme.

When I finished my remarks, the chamber was absolutely silent. I quickly turned and walked away from the lectern, my heart pounding. Had I really just said all that? Would it come back to haunt me somehow? It would be on TV and in all the newspapers, that much I knew. With a shock, I realized that I needed to call my dad, so he could hear it from me and not from news coverage. In making my spur-of-the-moment decision, I hadn't thought about the fact that I'd have to talk about this with Dad—and with my daughters, Sherry and Sydney, who were then just ten and eleven. My mother had passed in 2002, so she would never know about the assault.

After all the senators who wanted to speak had spoken, and the vote was finally taken, I was devastated to see that choosing to share my painful secret hadn't changed a damn thing. Every single Republican, and one Democrat, voted in favor of the bill, which meant I had pried myself open for nothing.

My disappointment flared into anger when a Republican senator approached me afterward and said, "I think you're really brave, and I wish I could have voted with you. My wife was raped in college too." All I could think was *How dare you walk up and say this to me, having cast the vote that you did?* It was one thing if people didn't comprehend what they were voting on. But here was a person who understood and still chose to vote the way that he did. What hope did we have?

After the vote, I hurried back to my office and called my father. "Dad, I just wanted you to know that I gave a speech on the floor, and it's going to be in the news, but I shared that I was raped in college." I felt mortified just blurting it out like that, but what choice did I have? Dad seemed deeply surprised, and he was upset for me, but he didn't seem sure of what to say. He and I have always been very close, so this was a strange and tough moment for us both.

In an ideal situation, I'd have been able to plan what to say ahead of time, to talk with him about it calmly and with some forethought. As it was, our conversation felt rushed and awkward. And let's be honest—no daughter really wants to talk about anything involving sex, or sexual violence, with her father. After keeping the assault secret for so long, it was a very difficult conversation to have.

I decided to tell the girls the next morning, as they were getting ready for school. I didn't want to get into a lot of detail, but I also didn't want them learning about it from school friends whose parents might have been discussing it. So I told them as forthrightly and calmly as I could that someone had hurt me in college and that it was in the news. They were upset, of course, and sad that their mom had been hurt. I told them that I was okay now, and if they ever had any questions about it, they could ask me anything.

Over the years, they did ask. And we were able to have good conversations about how to deal with the reality of rape, the aftermath, and how to help friends who might be going through something similar. The best way to help someone who reveals that they've been assaulted is to say "I'm sorry that happened to you" and "How can I support you?" My daughters hugged me and told me they loved me, and that was the best support I could have gotten.

As hard as it was to reveal publicly that I'd been raped, I eventually found catharsis in talking about it. I learned a lot about being a survivor and have encouraged other survivors to tell their stories, as long as they're comfortable doing so. But I've also learned that not everyone feels safe or able to talk about their trauma, and that's okay too. Everyone is different, and we all have to take our own path toward healing.

After I told my daughters that morning, I headed to work feeling hollowed-out and depressed. What had been the point of laying my soul bare in public, if the measure passed anyway? Then, during my drive, one of my staffers called. We had been inundated by emails and voicemails from people all over the country—and even as far away as Tunisia. My floor speech had been shared all over social media, and hundreds of people, including many who were survivors of assault themselves, had reached out to offer words of encouragement and thanks. It was a relief to realize that a moment I had feared was a waste had instead provided comfort, and might actually become a galvanizing force, for many women.

To my surprise, I was invited to appear on *The Rachel Maddow Show*—not usually something that happens to a state senator. In a short interview, I said we would keep fighting against the law and that I planned to introduce legislation to repeal it. "Considering the makeup of the legislature, I'm not optimistic that we'll get it through," I said, "but I am optimistic, because I know the people of this state are robustly against this legislation, and I believe if we go to the ballot, we can win. But it's a heavy lift, and we've got a big fight on our hands."

I wasn't wrong about that part. The fight would take years, but seeing the reaction of women to not just my story, but the stories and speeches of all who fought against that terrible law, was inspiring. I was determined not to give up until we got it off the books.

Over the next decade, we rolled up our sleeves and got to work. We passed a ballot initiative to draw fair districts, so gerrymandering—when legislators redraw voting districts to keep themselves in power—wouldn't artificially keep a minority party in power in perpetuity. When I won the governor's race in 2018, we used that momentum to strengthen the Democratic Party's infrastructure, leading to more electoral wins—including turning Michigan for Biden in 2020. And we galvanized voters who cared about reproductive freedom. In 2022, with a constitutional amendment to protect abortion rights on the ballot, voters came out in droves. For the first time since 1984, Democrats won the governorship, the Senate, and the House. With control of the legislature, we could finally repeal that terrible law.

On December 11, 2023, the ten-year anniversary of the day I made that floor speech, I once again stepped to the lectern in the Michigan State Senate. But this time, it wasn't to pry myself open or plead for Republicans to pay attention to the needs of women. It was to announce that as governor, I had just signed into law the final bill of the Reproductive Health Act, a new package of laws that would protect the rights of Michigan's women—and repeal the rape insurance law.

Wearing a fuchsia blazer, surrounded by women, I proudly announced that we were striking down the politically motivated and medically unnecessary laws and restoring personal freedoms for women.

"The moral of this story is, don't stop fighting for what you know is right," I went on. "There's a warning in the story, too, [to] anyone who wants to roll back our rights: Don't mess with American women. We're tough and we fight back and we will win. You come for our rights, and we will work harder to protect them." It was one of my proudest moments yet in politics.

When I think back to how depressed I felt after failing to sway the vote in 2013, I remember what a wise therapist once told me. "Everyone is a lump of clay," she said. "When a lump of clay is hollowed out, it becomes a cup, a vessel." I love the idea that when something is taken from you, what's left behind has a purpose. For a long time, I wanted to ignore the terrible event that had happened to me in college. But now I recognize that it also helped make me who I am, a woman who's willing to fight and not inclined to give up. I'll always be grateful that I could use that bad experience for good.

This chapter opened with a song that I can't bear to hear, and then it just got heavier from there . . . so let's close it out on a lighter note. I do love listening to music, so I've pulled together some of my favorite songs, if you want to give them a listen too. Turn the page for the True Gretch playlist.

TRUE GRETCH PLAYLIST

Song	Artist
Not Ready to Make Nice	The Chicks
Don't Stop Me Now	Queen
The Man	Taylor Swift
You Learn	Alanis Morissette
Welcome to the Jungle	Guns N' Roses
Seven Nation Army	The White Stripes
9 to 5	Dolly Parton
Top Knot Turn Up	Madame Gandhi
Think	Aretha Franklin
Born This Way	Lady Gaga
I'm Still Standing	Elton John
Fly as Me	Silk Sonic
Lose Yourself	Eminem
Formation	Beyoncé
The Fixer	Pearl Jam
Wrecking Ball	Miley Cyrus
Let's Go Crazy	Prince & The Revolution
Big Gretch	Gmac Cash

CHAPTER 3

LEARN TO LISTEN

When I was a kid, I wanted to grow up to be a sports broadcaster. As a student at Michigan State, I even had a part-time job working in the offices of the football program. But then my dad suggested I consider applying for an internship at the state capitol. "Not many people understand how government works," he told me. "You might decide you don't like politics, but an internship will give you knowledge that will help you navigate the world."

I took his advice to heart. And to my surprise, I fell in love with public policy. Working at the capitol, I learned how government can positively impact our lives every day, protecting the water we drink, the roads we travel, and the fundamental rights we share as humans. I went from never having thought about politics to watching close-up as legislators did the hard work that affected all of our lives.

Here's a thought exercise: What did you do when you woke up this morning? Your alarm went off, because a government-regulated utility provides you with affordable electricity. You ate a breakfast that didn't make you sick, because the government makes sure your food is safe. You brushed your teeth with clean water, then took a big yellow school bus on paved roads to school. If you stop to think about it, government services protect and enhance your life in dozens of ways every single day.

Unfortunately, when we hear the word "politics" today, it's hard not to picture people in opposite parties screaming at one another. But most of politics is finding ways to work together to help people. Part of my internship involved replying to constituents who'd reached out to ask for help. As I worked to find solutions to their problems, I realized that what good politics is *truly* about is making people's lives better. I was hooked.

During my first campaign for governor, in 2017–18, I went everywhere and met with everyone I possibly could. Michigan is made up of two peninsulas, nestled among the Great Lakes and home to a diverse population of ten million people. With my brother Richard driving, alternating between our two Ford SUVs, we racked up about 150,000 miles crisscrossing the state and meeting with anyone who was willing to take a few moments to chat.

One stop was at the Detroit Children's Hospital, where I asked doctors and administrators how the state could better help them with their needs and challenges. The meeting included a short tour of the facility, and as we walked past a sitting room, I could see a few patients and family members milling around. I decided to pop in and talk with them.

This was a hospital for children, so most people were there because of sad or difficult circumstances. They had very serious things going on in their lives, and I wasn't sure they'd be interested in chatting with a political candidate who happened to be passing through. That's one thing about life on the campaign trail—we're always going into places where we're not invited, and it can be awkward. Many candidates fill the void by prattling on about themselves and their platforms. But I didn't want to waste these people's time, so I decided instead to ask a direct question: What do you need?

The first person I approached was a young man named Cory, who'd recently had spinal surgery and was wearing a hospital gown. I made some small talk with him, then turned to his mother, a woman named Bridget Bonds. "If I'm fortunate enough to be the next governor of Michigan, what could I do to make your life better?" I asked. She looked me right in the eye and said, "I just need you to fix the damn roads."

That was not the answer I expected. Here's a mom with a son in the hospital, and she's focused on . . . roads? "Tell me more," I said. "Why is that the first thing on your mind?"

Bridget told me that she had two other sons, and that her family lived in Flint, about seventy miles from the hospital. She spent hours traveling back and forth every week to visit Cory, each time leaving her other kids in the care of a babysitter. One morning not long before, she'd hit a pothole on her way down to Detroit, and it had busted a rim on her car. This sidelined her for a whole day. She didn't get to visit Cory in the hospital and didn't get to be with her other sons at home. Instead, she spent those precious hours in an auto shop. That pothole had cost her not only a lot of money, but her valuable time.

Like so many others in Michigan—and particularly while driving those thousands of campaign miles with my brother—I had felt the pain of losing tires to potholes and seeing windshields crack from flying rocks. The state hadn't put any serious money into infrastructure in decades. And we get a lot of snow, so the cycle of freezing and thawing, freezing and thawing tended to leave the roads looking like Swiss cheese. For years, the state government did the absolute minimum to make the roads passable, filling potholes like a game of Whac-A-Mole and then just laying down more asphalt or concrete. That buys you a little bit of time, but it doesn't fix the underlying problem, that roads sometimes need to be rebuilt rather than just patched.

So, no matter where I went in Michigan, people were irritated about the roads. But it wasn't until Bridget shared her story in the hospital that day that the light bulb went on for me. Fixing the roads isn't just about giving people a smoother drive. It's about making sure people can take care of their families and get to work and the grocery store and the ballgame and the barbecue. It's about not having to waste hours of your life that you should be able to spend with your kids. It's about what's lost when a pothole gobbles up your tire, your money, and your time.

When Bridget said "fix the damn roads" that day, I could have just nodded my head and moved on to the next person. I had probably done that at other events. But because I followed up to ask why the roads were her biggest concern, I now understood the issue in a deeper way. Fixing the roads wasn't about roads. It was about life.

Back out on the campaign trail, I started using the phrase in my speeches. After a while, my campaign manager, Eric Goldman, asked, "How do you feel about running on that?" I wasn't sure, but Eric pointed out that this was exactly how people talked about the roads, so we took a chance and made it our official slogan—without even testing or polling on it. We printed up literature, sent out mailings, even wrapped buses with the words. We drove all over the state on a "Fix the Damn Roads" bus tour, and pretty soon, people were yelling the phrase whenever I stepped up to speak.

Everybody loved the slogan . . . except for those who didn't. A few people were offended by the word "damn," saying that kids shouldn't have to listen to such language on TV. I thought, *Well, damn.* The president of the United States had been elected after clips went viral of him bragging that he could "grab 'em by the pussy." Our slogan was mild in comparison, it wasn't disparaging, and it gave voice to the frustration people felt. We were tackling a problem, not attacking people. So we decided to keep it.

Oh, and besides that—it worked. My campaign took off, and

on election day, I beat my Republican opponent by almost ten points. I invited Bridget Bonds to introduce me at my inauguration on New Year's Day of 2019, which she graciously agreed to do, even though as a committed Christian lady, she swears that she didn't say the word "damn" when we spoke that day at the hospital. She may be right, and it's admittedly kind of funny if my story about listening involves mishearing someone. But the sentiment was definitely there, and judging from what she said at the inauguration, Bridget felt like she and Cory were heard.

"Of all the registered voters in the room, I can remember her going up to my son and asking him what he would like to see change from the new governor," she said. "Out of all the people in the room, the fact that she went up to my son, it touched my heart."

• • • •

I first realized how important listening was when I was very young and having a hard time, and someone important took time to listen to me. Her name was Sylvia Buie, and she was my second-grade teacher.

My mom and dad got divorced when I was six. I can remember hearing them yelling at each other and Dad leaving the house. I felt so sad for him, because he had to go off and live by himself, while we stayed with Mom at the house that had been his home too.

As the oldest child, I felt responsible for making sure my little sister and brother were okay. The divorce was fresh and raw, and my parents were struggling to communicate, so I ended up as the go-between, relaying messages from one to the other about when someone was supposed to pick us up, or when each parent would be spending time with us. I turned into a caregiver at an age when kids should be carefree.

I used to walk Liz to school every morning, but because she was in kindergarten, she'd leave to go home after a half day. Since second graders stayed through the afternoon, I couldn't go with her, and I felt paralyzed with worry about whether she'd make it home safe. Each lunchtime, I'd get distracted and withdrawn because I knew she was walking alone. It's not that we lived so far away, or that the walk was dangerous. It's that I felt scared and unsure in general. Life had thrown a curveball at me, and nothing felt safe anymore.

Ms. Buie noticed my distress, and she sat me down after class one day to ask what was going on. I remember feeling surprised, because in my very limited experience, adults didn't have real conversations with kids. I'd never had a teacher— or any grown-up, other than my parents—ask me how I was doing, then sit patiently and listen. Ms. Buie had a big, warm smile, but what I remember most is how she sat quietly, watching me steadily as I tried to put into words what I was feeling. The next day, she arranged for me to walk Liz home, so I could see that she would be okay. It helped.

I'm grateful to Ms. Buie not only for helping soothe my second-grade self, but for teaching me by example the importance of listening. I've had plenty of experiences (particularly with politicians) where the person talking to you keeps glancing around the room to see if anyone more important is nearby. I know how it feels, so I don't do it to others. No matter who I'm meeting with, from students to presidents, I make a point of looking them in the eye and giving them my undivided focus. As I learned with Ms. Buie, an unremarkable moment in one person's day might feel like a life-changing event for another.

Liz grew up to be a pretty good listener too (no doubt from the wonderful influence of her big sister). She talks about a theory she learned in business school called "the five whys," which is basically about digging deeper to understand a problem. If someone tells you, "I'm uncomfortable with gay marriage," you might be tempted to shut down the conversation. Or you could ask why, and then listen. Let the person speak, take it in, and then ask more questions. And keep asking why, like an annoying three-year-old. You won't always find your way to an agreement. But you are more likely to get to the root of the person's feelings, and that's a start.

As a freshman legislator, I was one of very few women on the appropriations committee, which prioritizes and makes spending decisions for the state government. The governor at the time proposed cutting a line in the health budget that provided cervical cancer screening for poor women.

"Why would we cut this?" I asked. The answer I got was that people hadn't been utilizing it, so the governor wanted to put the money elsewhere. Simple enough, right? Why throw away the state's dollars on something no one wants?

But something wasn't adding up; it made no sense that people wouldn't take advantage of a free service. So I pushed further. "It's not like poor women aren't at risk of cervical cancer," I said, "so why aren't they using it?" This was the question behind the question. And it didn't take much digging to find the answer. The sad truth is, when people know they can't afford cancer treatment, they often prefer not to know if they have it. That was the real problem. So instead of defunding the testing program, I worked to get the bill amended to provide treatment for women who learned they had cancer. And lo and behold, women started getting tested.

I always try to find the question behind the question—and sometimes it saves me from embarrassment. Once, during a campaign, someone asked me, "Are you going to run as a woman?" I thought, *As opposed to what? I mean, I am a woman, so do I have a choice here?* My first reaction was to laugh. But I managed to get ahold of myself and instead asked what he meant. It turned out that what he wanted to know was whether I planned to focus only on "women's issues" like abortion rights and pay equity—an earnest question.

So, yes. I did run as a woman, but not only as a woman. And at that moment, I was running as a woman who felt fortunate not to have put her foot in her mouth.

Listening to people has served me very well, and as governor I've tried to ensure that people truly feel heard. In early 2021, after the January 6 attack on the US Capitol, and with Michiganders still feeling raw about the pandemic stay-at-home orders, I wanted to get out into communities where it seemed like people didn't feel heard and listen to what they had to say. We decided to call this the "Fix the Damn Road Ahead" tour.

We planned roundtable events in counties across Michigan, contacting random residents who might have been interested in sharing their thoughts. When you're governor, it can be hard to have real conversations with your constituents. People get nervous, and sometimes, given the amount of orchestration and security involved, interactions can feel forced. We wanted people to feel as comfortable as possible, so we set up the events in backyards, with folding chairs and a relaxed vibe.

One of the roundtables took place in Midland, where we gathered local farmers and agricultural workers to ask how they felt about what was happening in the state. In general, farmers tend to be pretty conservative. "Tell me what it's like for you right now," I said. "What problems are you dealing with? How can we help?"

Farming has never been an easy way to make a living, and with the pandemic, climate change, difficulty in finding agricultural workers, and a thousand other problems, I knew these farmers were at a crisis point. I expected to hear about these issues and to get an earful about the stay-at-home orders and other measures I had put in place to keep Michiganders safe. I'd taken these steps in hopes of saving lives, but they had taken a toll on people. Most just buckled down and dealt with the inconveniences as best they could. But some had been so infuriated that they began showing up at my house, guns in hand, to protest. So I braced myself for the torrent that was surely coming.

One man started talking about how his family had been farming for generations, and that he personally had been doing it for decades. And then he said something that surprised me. "It used to be that when I drove my combine down a two-lane road, people would swing out to let me pass, slow down, and wave." People used to be friendly, he went on. "Now, they honk and swear and flip me off." We used to have a basic level of decency, but now that decency was gone, and it made him feel disheartened.

As I listened to the farmer, I thought about how this man, in this rural part of the state, was feeling the same kind of ugliness that I was feeling in Lansing, and that people from all walks of life were feeling in Detroit and Grand Rapids and Marquette. Despite our divisions, we had this common thread. And while there was no easy path to fixing the problem, the first step was obvious, and we were doing it. We asked, and we listened, and we let this farmer know that he was heard.

Hearing these stories helped make me a better communicator and a more effective governor. And you know what the funny part of it is? Every time we hold one of these roundtables, people seem surprised that I'm sitting there and listening to them, taking notes and keeping my mouth shut. With politicians that doesn't happen very often, but it should. It feels like a magical tool in the toolbox—a way to connect with people and come away feeling energized and confident that I'm focusing on the right things.

A NOTE ON NOTES

Speaking of magical tools, I have two others that I count on. They're real throwbacks, but still effective.

As anybody on my staff can tell you, I have a thing about taking notes. I'm always telling people to bring a pen and paper everywhere, and I'm never without them myself. Computers and recorders are fine, but there's something about good old-fashioned handwritten notes that floats my boat. I learned over the years that writing something down is the best way to imprint it on my brain.

The habit originated with my dad, who was a dedicated pen-and-paper guy. Whenever we have an important conversation, Dad still comes to the table armed with a yellow legal pad and a black felt-tip Flair pen. If we were in trouble, he'd already have an outline written on it. When we got in trouble as teenagers, he never raised his voice but would just say quietly that we needed to have a talk—and if we saw that outline, we knew we were toast.

Every year for Christmas, Dad gave each of us personalized notepads on colorful paper, with our names, and best of all, little sketches we'd drawn. Sometimes they were self-portraits, although Liz for some reason liked to draw clowns. (Actually, maybe those were self-portraits?) Liz used her pads to write short plays that we'd perform, and I used mine for writing notes, sometimes for friends and sometimes for my dad.

Dad would write little notes for us, too, and he always signed them the same way: "LLLD"—for Love, Love, Love, Dad.

CHAPTER 4

SURROUND YOURSELF WITH GREAT PEOPLE—AND DON'T BE AFRAID TO ASK FOR HELP

In late January of 2019, just three weeks after taking the oath of office, I faced my first crisis as governor when a polar vortex descended on Michigan. As a mass of Arctic air swept down from the North Pole, our state plunged from its usual cold-but-bearable winter into an icy, treacherous, subzero nightmare.

Michiganders are a hardy bunch, but this wasn't weather you could just muscle your way through. As heavy snow fell, the wind whipped temperatures down to record lows. A slippery sheen of ice covered the roads, and multicar pileups were happening on the highways. On Monday, January 28, with forecasts predicting windchills down to minus fifty, I declared a state of emergency so we would have more resources for relief and response. We were going to need them.

Businesses closed; airplanes were grounded; schools shut down. The postal service stopped delivering, and my alma mater, Michigan State, canceled classes for only the seventh time in its then-164-year history. We urged people to stay at home, and for the most part they did. But now all the houses and apartment buildings across Michigan were cranking up their heat at the same time, which was putting a lot of stress on the utility companies.

That Wednesday, with the state mired in subzero temperatures, we got a shocking call. Consumers Energy, one of Michigan's biggest utilities, had suffered a fire at their compressor station in Macomb County, and there was a risk that the station would go down entirely. If that happened, about a million people could lose their power, and more important, their heat. This was not some minor inconvenience. In these kinds of temperatures, a lack of heat could lead to hundreds, maybe thousands, of deaths.

My team and I rushed to the State Emergency Operations Center (SEOC) in Dimondale, where officials from emergency management, the Michigan Public Service Commission, and local first responders were working on the problem. But there was no obvious solution: we couldn't change the weather, and it was going to take time for Consumers Energy to fix the damage at the station.

We were in constant contact with their top officials, who warned us that between nine and ten a.m. the next day, when energy usage would be at its peak, the demand for natural gas would exceed supply—which meant that pilot lights across Michigan would go out. Unlike with electrical failures, the company couldn't just turn everything back on when it was over.

We were looking at the possibility of having to deploy the Michigan National Guard to help people reignite their pilot lights.

This was a disaster waiting to happen. We had to find a way to lower demand. Consumers Energy had already asked their business customers to lower their usage, either by shutting for the day or by turning down their thermostats. If that wasn't enough to stem the demand, the company might have to implement rolling blackouts.

No one liked the idea of shutting off anyone's power, but we were running out of options. Then someone made a suggestion: Instead of cutting off service, why not ask people to voluntarily lower their thermostats? If enough homes turned down their heat, there was a chance we could keep the electricity on for everyone. We would be asking Michiganders to help, and trusting them to do the right thing. And we wouldn't need 100 percent compliance, just enough to tip the scales.

At ten p.m., I spoke at a press conference. "I'm coming to you now to ask for your help," I said, then asked everyone who was able to turn down their thermostats. "You can play a role in helping people across the state survive these extreme temperatures," I said. "Please do. We're calling on every Michigander to do your part and help us weather this storm together."

We hoped this would be effective, but because it was so late already, many people were going to bed or already asleep. So we also took the unusual move of using the state alert system to send a message to cell phones and interrupt TV broadcasts.

At ten thirty p.m., every cell phone in Michigan pinged with this message: "Emergency Alert: Due to extreme temps Consumers asks everyone to lower their heat to 65 or less through Fri." And you know what? People did it. They threw extra blankets on their beds, put on their parkas and wool hats indoors, and saved the whole grid from going down. We got through the night without anyone losing power, and the next day the compressor station was back online. High five, Michigan!

When I think about this story, a couple of takeaways come to mind. One is the simple fact that if you ask people to help, more often than not they'll do it. And the other is that it pays to surround yourself with great people. In a frantic situation, with officials weighing in from all sides, my team members stepped up with great suggestions for how to solve this crisis. I always aim to hire people who have skill sets or perspectives I lack, because you get a lot more accomplished if you surround yourself with people who make you better.

I'll talk more about my team in a moment, but first, a quick flashback to a younger, messier, and—well, let's call it a less enlightened time of my life.

As a young teenager, I was still trying to figure out where I fit in. My middle school years had been a bit chaotic, since we moved from East Lansing to Grand Rapids just before I started fifth grade. Moving from our hometown to a new place, where I didn't know anyone, was a huge adjustment. On top of that, we were now living with my mom and stepdad, and we had a new stepbrother. It felt like the ground was shifting beneath me.

I tried to make the best of my situation, running for fifth-grade class secretary, but I lost overwhelmingly, epically. My dad came to hear my campaign speech, and he comforted me after I lost, but it was hard not to feel rejected by my new classmates. I just felt out of place, and my clumsiness didn't help matters. On the day we took our class photos, a bunch of girls were doing their hair with brush curling irons, and when I borrowed one, I managed to get my long hair twisted up so badly, we had to cut a chunk out. *Whoops!* I sucked it up and smiled for the photos, but I was dying a little inside.

The next year, I started middle school. And because three elementary schools fed into one middle school, I was no longer the only person who was in class with a bunch of kids I didn't know. That was a relief, but an embarrassing moment in class one day felt like another setback.

"Gretchen," my teacher said out of the blue, "you may be excused to go to the nurse." *What?* I thought. *Why?* She explained quietly to me that I had bled through the pants I was wearing that day—of course, they had to be *white* pants. I was so shocked; this was my first period, and while I knew it would happen, I hadn't expected it that soon. I walked out of the classroom, holding my Trapper Keeper folder behind me, and hustled down the hallway to the nurse's office.

So, life at school wasn't super smooth. And neither was life at home.

Before the move to Grand Rapids, my mom and I had gotten along fine. After the move, we started clashing. She was upset with me because I wasn't a disciplined student and wasn't making good grades. "You're not applying yourself!" she'd say. And she wasn't wrong. But I didn't feel challenged, and there weren't any teachers I particularly connected with. By the time I started ninth grade at Forest Hills Central High School, I was still floundering, trying out different friend groups and attempting to figure out where I belonged. It's easy to get pigeonholed as one thing in high school, either a jock or a nerd or a partier—as if anyone is just one thing. I settled in with the fast crowd and became known as a partier.

One Friday night during my sophomore year, I went with some friends to a football game, and we drank so much that I ended up passing out in the parking lot. Although tailgating is a great Michigan tradition, that's clearly a bit much for a fifteen-year-old. But the story gets worse.

The principal happened to find me between two parked cars as he was strolling through the parking lot. And while I'd like to say that I gathered myself enough to walk away with dignity, I actually threw up on him. Sorry, Mr. Bleke! He called my mom, who came to pick me up and was already raging when I crawled miserably into the car. At home, she threw me into the shower to sober me up and then told me I was grounded for a month. Mom was the kind of person who yelled when she was mad—which I didn't enjoy, but at least I was used to it. When I saw my dad, though, he just sat down with his yellow legal pad and an outline, ready for the talk. That's when I felt awful, not just physically but emotionally now too.

It was a rough weekend. Then, that Monday morning, I was sitting in first period when the classroom phone rang. My teacher answered, looked at me, hung up, and said, "Miss Whitmer, Mr. Bleke would like you to come to the office." Of course, everybody had heard what had happened at the game, so the whole class went "Ooooooh!" I collected my things and slunk from the classroom to the office, where the principal told me I was suspended for three days. Once again, my mother had to come pick me up, and now I was in for another three days of getting an earful from my angry mom. This was the first time in my life when, if given the choice between being at home or at school, I'd have gladly chosen school.

After that, I began trying to get my act together. I was embarrassed, and I didn't like being grounded. I'd been meandering along through school and life, but that clearly wasn't working. I had always wanted to go to Michigan State, but now I realized that if I continued down this path, I'd never get accepted there.

In my junior year, I buckled down, and that spring I received the most improved student award. I applied to MSU, and to my relief I got in—an outcome that hadn't seemed possible the year before. And while I continued to enjoy a robust social life in college, I had some remarkable professors who recognized the student behind the partier. I spent time in office hours with one in particular, Professor Steve McCornack, who helped me see the possibilities of what I could do with my life.

There's nothing wrong with having a good time, and I made some great friends in high school and college, but it wasn't until I went to law school in my mid-twenties that I found myself surrounded by ambitious, smart peers who were serious about making their mark in the world. That's when I realized that I wanted to make a mark too, even if I wasn't sure yet how to do it. Suddenly I found myself in a competitive, engaging environment, studying subjects that fascinated me. And because law school classes were taught by the Socratic method, where you might get called on at any time, I was always on my toes. It was a fun and exciting time.

I had decided to go to law school because, coming from a family of lawyers, I knew that degree came with a lot of options. My uncle was a prosecutor, my aunt was a judge, my dad was a business executive, and my mother was an assistant attorney general who fought to protect consumers in Michigan. Every one of them had a different job, but their law degrees had prepared them for those paths. And now I've used my degree to help me become an effective legislator and governor.

I first ran for the State House in 2000, two years after graduating with honors from Michigan State College of Law. When I won that race, I hired the best people I could find for my staff of three. One of those hires, Nancy Bohnet, is still with me twenty-four years later. In fact, I've had a lot of staffers stay with me for a decade or more. And most of my top people now have been with me for both terms of my governorship. They all know so many things I don't, and I lean on them for expertise and advice.

It pays to have smart and motivated people, but also to ask for help from people who know stuff you don't. That's certainly true for me in one particular realm that I know nothing about: social media.

It is objectively true (in my subjective opinion) that I have the most creative social media of any of the governors. My social media team makes me look good every single day, even—or maybe especially—when they're making me look silly.

Our digital and creative director, Julia Pickett, has gotten us millions of views on TikTok and Instagram by making funny and smart short videos. She's made hilarious blooper reels, had me do a fashion show with leather jackets (my preferred armor), and even turned me into a talking potato. Whenever one of our posts goes viral, I also get the side benefit of saying to my daughters, "Wow, I just can't stop trending!" Seeing their eyes roll always makes my day.

Julia is young and fearless, and while the rest of the team weighs in so we don't do anything too nuts, we absolutely push the envelope. I want my team to be creative and stretch the limits of what we do. And once a decision is made, I'll do pretty much whatever they ask me to. Because they know more about how social media works than I ever will.

The best example of their genius is Lil' Gretch. In July of 2023, as excitement was building for Greta Gerwig's upcoming *Barbie* movie, Julia pitched the idea of creating a Barbie governor doll, fashioned after me and dressed in hot pink—my favorite color and one I wear all the time. She bought an America Ferrera Barbie, then gave her a haircut like mine (a much better one than the haircuts I used to give my "weird" Barbies as a kid) and proposed putting her behind a little podium or driving around in a toy car.

I loved the idea that little Governor Barbie could sign legislation and explain political issues. In fact, we decided this was the perfect way to educate people about the state's budget. Because the budget is thousands of pages long and often contains bureaucratic jargon, most people consider it boring. But the budget changes lives, distributing funding for all the things that improve our everyday existence—so why not connect it to a pop culture moment, to reach a whole new generation of Michiganders who might not otherwise be paying attention? "Let's do it!" I said, and my team got to work.

Julia built a tiny wooden podium, and we created a series of photos and videos with Lil' Gretch in my ceremonial office in the capitol. She also bought a toy pink Corvette and took photos of Lil' Gretch tooling around with the top down.

Everybody on the team cracked up. This was a brilliant, fun

way to catch the wave of Barbie excitement that was sweeping the country. Then my chief communications officer, Kaylie Hanson, took it a step further, pitching *The New York Times* to do a story about it. That piece, which came out on July 20, 2023, included tons of information not only about Lil' Gretch, but about women in politics and the work my administration had done for women's rights. This was a slam dunk, a positive piece that brought some joy and laughter amid grim political times.

Our "Governor Barbie" campaign ran on X/Twitter, Instagram, TikTok, Threads, and Facebook, getting five million impressions across platforms. It won a 2023 Shorty Impact Award for best social media in the Government and Politics category, and then a Webby award in 2024. Most important, it got our message out to millions of people in a fun and lighthearted way. And that's all thanks to the team of great people who not only knew what they were doing but were willing to stretch creatively.

Times change, and the truth is, you can't solve every problem the way it was solved in the past. Granted, trying something new doesn't always work. Sometimes you catch fire, like Lil' Gretch, and sometimes you catch heat, like when the team turned me into a potato—not my best look. But one thing is certain: there's no great success without risk. So just accept that not everything will go perfectly. That's okay! It's still worth trying.

Lil' Gretch tooling around in her pink Corvette.

(Left) *You know I must trust my team to let them turn me into a potato.* (Right) *Lil' Gretch telling it like it is.*

Here's another truth about problem-solving. It pays to have a diversity of people in the room, because everyone brings a different kind of experience to the table. In the early 1980s, when NASA was preparing to send one of the first female American astronauts, Sally Ride, into space, they planned to send her with one hundred tampons—for a six-day trip. For anyone reading this who might not know, that's *way* more than she'd need. NASA would have known that if they'd had any women at the table planning the mission.

I'll give you another example, from closer to home.

When the Covid pandemic started in early 2020, thirty-seven other states reported cases before we got our first one in Michigan. But once we had it, the virus tore through our cities and towns, particularly metro Detroit. By the end of March— the same month I was locked in a battle of words and wills with President Trump, trying to get supplies for our state—Michigan had the third-highest number of Covid-related deaths, behind only New York and New Jersey.

How did this happen in just three weeks? Why were we getting hit so hard, and what could we do to stem the spread? Fortunately for us, we had Dr. Joneigh Khaldun—better known as Dr. J—to help answer these questions. The first Black chief medical executive in Michigan's history, she joined my team in 2019, and when our first Covid cases were identified, she became a constant adviser even as she continued to practice emergency room medicine in Detroit. Dr. J wasn't just sitting in an office, trying to figure out how the virus might impact Michiganders. She was seeing what was happening on the ground.

We didn't have much data early in the pandemic, as things were moving too quickly and chaotically. But because Dr. J was on the front lines in Detroit, she saw immediately that the virus was hitting the Black community disproportionately hard. As the numbers later showed, African Americans made up 40 percent of our early deaths, even though Black Michiganders represent just 14 percent of the population in our state.

Dr. J didn't wait for the official data that would prove what she was seeing with her own eyes. She told me, "We need to do outreach. Right now." We worked with medical professionals, faith leaders, and community leaders to get information out, and Dr. J was always by my side at our frequent press conferences to talk about the pandemic. I wanted people to see her and hear her message, in hopes that we could get the word into our most vulnerable communities about how to keep the virus at bay.

Over an eight-week period, I issued sixty-nine executive orders in an effort to slow the spread of the virus, including the "stay home, stay safe" executive order, which required people to remain in their homes or, if they absolutely had to be out, at least six feet away from others.

At first, we had bipartisan support for these moves. But after my beef with Trump, Republicans began pushing back—and so did their conservative constituents, who became more and more vocal about what they saw as unfair restrictions. Now, in addition to fighting a pandemic, we had a culture war brewing. Black Americans were suffering and dying in disproportionate numbers, while other pockets of Michiganders were angry about losing their "freedom." And then everything boiled over.

On April 8, we reached a terrible milestone, becoming the third state to record more than twenty thousand cases. Desperate to stem the virus's spread, I extended the stay-at-home order for three more weeks. This further inflamed some people's tempers, but I knew we had no choice. It was my duty to protect all the citizens of my state, and with cases spiking, I didn't have time to worry about whether it would make some angry or upset.

I would end up extending the stay-at-home order multiple times, keeping much of Michigan at home until late May, despite the increasingly vocal opposition. I'm not the only governor who did this, of course. Others did too, and many of us—both Republicans and Democrats—stayed in close contact, working together to help one another find needed supplies.

My efforts to save Michiganders' lives resulted in threats to my own. But there were many in Michigan who had my back, because they sensed that I had theirs. The Black community, which had been hit so hard by the pandemic, stepped up to support me just when I needed it.

We would often livestream our press conferences on social

media, and at some point the name Big Gretch started popping up in the comments. People were writing things like "Big Gretch is looking out for us" and "Big Gretch said shut it DOWN!" I was doing a thousand things at once during that period and never saw the comments or the nickname. But a rapper named Gmac Cash did, and he decided to put it to music.

On May 2, he released a music video for the song "Big Gretch," complete with a photoshopped image of me wearing sunglasses.

> On behalf of Detroit
> We want to present these Buffs to our governor,
>   Big Gretch!

> Throw the Buffs on her face, 'cause that's Big
>   Gretch
> We ain't even 'bout to stress, we got Big Gretch
> You can find her in the press under "Big Gretch"
> Fresh in a new dress, yeah, that's Big Gretch . . .

> Big Gretch in this bitch, playin' no roles (at all)
> Excuse all the cussin', that's just how I get my flow
>   on (for real)
> If you wanna leave the state, you can stay gone
> But right now, Big Gretch says, "Stay home" (sit
>   your ass down)

One of my staffers played the song for me, and, I have to be honest, I wasn't sure what to think. Was this a good thing? What were Buffs? And who wants to be called "big," anyway? Gmac Cash didn't know this, of course, but I never liked to be called Gretch. My Grandma Gretchen always used to tell me, "Your name is Gretchen. Gretchen is a pretty name. Gretch is not a pretty word." As my brother Richard recently, and correctly, pointed out, "If I had ever called you Big Gretch growing up, you would have murdered me."*

So at first, I didn't know how I should feel about the song. Then one of my senior aides, Shaquila Myers, came to my rescue. A Detroit native, Shaquila said, "Oh, you don't understand. This is the highest compliment you can get! The people have accepted you!" She explained that Buffs are high-end Cartier buffalo-horn sunglasses, a status symbol in Detroit, especially among hip-hop artists and athletes. When Gmac Cash rapped that Detroit wanted to "present these Buffs to our governor," it was meant as an honor, to thank me for being "on the lookout" for them.

Gmac set up a GoFundMe to get me my own pair of Buffs, and more than two hundred people chipped in. I was touched by this show of support, and although the gift would have been legal under Michigan law, I just didn't feel comfortable

_____

* As you can tell by the title of this book, I've learned to embrace "Gretch." Sorry, Grandma Gretchen!

accepting a pair of $2,500 sunglasses. I asked Gmac to donate the money to charity instead, so $2,950 went to a group called New Era Detroit, which planned to use it to feed families in the community.

I might never own a pair of real Buffs, but I was grateful to Gmac Cash and Detroiters for expressing support for what I was doing. "Big Gretch" came out in a scary and stressful time for me, when the president of the United States was singling me out and some people in my state were sending me death threats. Getting an infusion of love and support from the people of Detroit at that moment meant more than I can say.

"This is too much," I tweeted after the song came out. "Love the nickname. Love the song. See ya at the cookout, Gmac Cash. Until then, Big Gretch says stay home and stay safe."

I'll always be grateful to Dr. J for helping us see the disproportionate impact of Covid on Michigan's communities of color. In that case, having a diversity of voices at the table not only led to greater understanding. It also saved lives.

CHAPTER 5

TAKE NOTHING PERSONALLY

Because I opened this book with one grandmother, Nino, it's only fair to share a little bit about the other one, Grandma Gretchen. Lucky for you, she was a hoot.

Grandma Gretchen, my mom's mother, was a tiny woman with long salt-and-pepper hair, dark eyes, and olive skin. It's funny that I'm named after her, because I turned out to be the only one of the Whitmer kids who looks like her. Both Richard and Liz are fair and blond, and I'm the outlier, a brown-eyed brunette. So I loved our trips to go visit Grandma Gretchen down in Bradenton, Florida.

She had a bike gang in Bradenton—not motorcycles, but a group of feisty, fun women who'd ride their bikes to McDonald's for breakfast a couple of days a week. She'd wear a crocheted hat with a pom-pom on top and a little wig fringe hanging off the back, so she didn't have to do her hair. And then she'd ride off on her Schwinn, her purse in the front basket, to meet her friends. She always put on lipstick, did her nails, and wore clothes that flattered her petite figure, even into her nineties.

One year when I was in college, I went with a bunch of friends down to Florida for spring break. We had a place for a week, which was one night short of our planned eight-day trip. With nowhere else to stay, we all piled into Grandma Gretchen's two-bedroom mobile home for that last night. It happened to be during March Madness, and she sat in front of the TV, watching games with her filled-out bracket, a goblet of beer, and a slice of pepperoni pizza. "Uh, your grandmother is cool," one of my friends said, awestruck. Yep. She definitely was.

All of her grandkids loved spending time with her, because she'd scratch our heads with her long red fingernails and sometimes treat us to dinner at the "Red Lobster House" (as she called it). For Christmas, she always gave us those little individually wrapped Andes mints and would let us choose from a grab bag of gifts. But my favorite thing she did, and the reason I'm telling you about her, is this: she'd pull you into a tight hug and whisper into your ear, "You're my favorite child." And as she was doing that, she'd be winking over your shoulder at whoever else was nearby and mouthing, *You are!*

This cracked us up every time. Everybody always wants to be their grandma's favorite kid. Grandma Gretchen did us one better, though—she let us in on the joke.

Grandma Gretchen

Because we all learned at an early age not to take ourselves too seriously, we're also pretty good at not taking things personally. This turns out to be a particularly useful skill when you're a public figure. Or, as I unfortunately discovered during my first term as governor, when your figure becomes a matter of public discussion.

About six weeks after the inauguration, it was time to deliver the State of the State address. My staff and I worked hard on the speech, which was my first opportunity to lay out a plan for what we were going to accomplish for Michigan. Both the House and Senate were majority-Republican, so I knew it wouldn't be the friendliest audience. I wanted to nail this speech, to show confidence as a newly elected governor and chart a path forward for fixing our (damn) roads, cleaning up our drinking water, securing rights for the LGBTQ+ community, and improving our education system.

In the days leading up to the speech, I got a couple of dresses from Rent the Runway. While men can wear the same two suits for years, just mixing them up with different color shirts and ties, women need a full wardrobe of different outfits—and that can get expensive. So I decided to rent something, ultimately choosing a bright blue dress that was almost identical in style to a dark red one I'd worn on election night three months before.

The night of the speech, I felt great. The House chamber in Michigan's capitol is a grand, historic space, decorated in teal and gold, with a huge coat of arms over the Speaker's chair and original wooden desks from 1878. I took my place at the elevated rostrum, looked out over the packed chamber, and began to speak. And whoops—no one could hear me. "Oh, I gotta turn it on," I said, and flipped the switch. Minor snafu there, hopefully the only thing that would go wrong that night.

I spoke for nearly an hour, finishing up with a message about bipartisanship. "We all have families. We all care about our kids' and our grandkids' futures. We all want what's best for our communities and our state," I said. "It's important for us to remember that the enemy is not the person across the aisle. The enemy is apathy. The enemy is extreme partisanship. The enemy is self-interest."

As I caught the eyes of my girls and my husband in the front row, I delivered my final lines: "The question is, do we have the wisdom to put partisanship aside and get the job done for the people we serve? I think we do. So, let's get to work." The chamber erupted in applause, and I left the rostrum feeling invigorated. The speech had gone as well as I could have hoped. We got all the important stuff right.

Then the fashion police showed up. The following evening, the Detroit Fox News affiliate aired a story on . . . my dress. Or rather, on the comments people had made about it, and more specifically about my body, on Fox 2's Facebook page. A (female!) reporter deemed this a topic of such vital interest, she went around interviewing people on the street about it, taking care to pepper her report with the most obnoxious comments from social media.

The comments Fox 2 chose to highlight read like a giant sexist haiku:

"Dress is looking a little tight."
"I'd hit it."
"Push-up bra, clearly."
"Look how tight it is on her arms."
"Heavy up top."

And then, chef's kiss, this bit:

"Some Facebook users also asked if her breasts are real, with posts asking what size they are. One man said, 'nice rack,' and another [said] 'She's showing off her cans. Why not? You got it? Share it.'"

My . . . cans? Seriously?

Until this report came out, I had felt pretty good about my speech. Any serious commentary about its content was generally positive, and I hadn't given a second thought to what I'd worn while delivering it. But when I watched this report about people criticizing my body, I was hurt. Not because people didn't think I looked good—I don't care about that. It was because I was trying to do something good, and met with a torrent of demoralizing, superficial sexist commentary.

Once again, as with the "rape insurance" rider, my thoughts went to my daughters, Sydney and Sherry. They were teenagers now, and here was an in-your-face reminder of the kind of BS they'd have to deal with as young women, and the hurdles women still face. Just three months earlier, Michigan voters had elected women to serve as our state's governor, attorney general, and secretary of state. Our new chief justice of the Supreme Court was a woman. The 2018 elections were dubbed the "Year of the Woman." And still we continue to have to deal with this kind of crap.

The next day, I posted three tweets about the report:

Governor Gretchen Whitmer ✔
@GovWhitmer

Boys have teased me about my curves since 5th grade. My mom said "hold your head high and don't let it bother you."

That @Fox2News story was way out of line.

I'm tough, I can take it.

3:17 PM · Feb 14, 2019

718 Reposts   **209** Quotes   **5,967** Likes   **17** Bookmarks

Governor Gretchen Whitmer ✔
@GovWhitmer

In my speech I was encouraging people to see the humanity in one another in this cruel political environment. In an era when so many women are stepping up to lead, I'm hoping people will focus on our ideas and accomplishments instead of our appearance.

3:17 PM · Feb 14, 2019

286 Reposts   **19** Quotes   **2,487** Likes   **1** Bookmark

Governor Gretchen Whitmer ✔
@GovWhitmer

Until then, I've got a message for all of the women and girls like mine who have to deal with garbage like this every day: I've got your back.

3:17 PM · Feb 14, 2019

411 Reposts   **63** Quotes   **3,907** Likes   **1** Bookmark

It's important to remember that most of the time, when someone says something nasty about you, it says more about them than you. The simple truth is it's exhausting to be a woman in society, because we're the ones who have to do the mental gymnastics about how to respond to unkind, unwarranted comments. We have to ask ourselves, *Is this someone I can educate? Or is it better to ignore them? Can I laugh it off?* We end up spending all this energy, just because someone decided to make a cruel or unkind comment.

Fox 2 ended up getting flak from all sides, including conservative outlets such as *The Washington Times* and even the Republican Speaker of the Michigan House, who called the piece "ridiculous." The reporter defended herself by saying she was only trying to highlight the serious problem of trolls on social media. *How?* I thought. *By amplifying and rewarding them?* Ultimately, Fox 2 seems to have taken down the report, because the link on their site leads to a blank page. That's too bad, for only one reason. There was a moment in it that ended up making me laugh and feel better—which brings me back around to Grandma Gretchen and learning not to take things personally.

It was an interview with a middle-aged white guy in a hoodie and knit hat. "She kinda looked like she was pregnant a little bit," he told the reporter. *Really?* I thought. *Now, there's a double standard for you.* His comment reminded me how ridiculous this whole situation was, and in that moment I realized it was better just to laugh and move on. Sometimes there's no way around the muck and stupidity—you just have to get through it. Seeing the absurdity always helps.

No matter how many times it happens, I'm somehow always surprised at the things people are willing to say not only about me, but to me. Some of them are meant as compliments

(I think?), but my God, the way they come out. Once, I was door-knocking during a Senate campaign, and a man answered in his bathrobe. After looking me up and down, he said, "Huh. You look much bigger on television." It was clear that he meant this as a compliment—that I was more to his liking in person—so I said, "Thank you?" Which is really all you can say in these situations.

Similarly, a woman said to me not long ago, "Oh, I am so glad you're buying better bras!" At my confused look, she went on, "You don't remember, but I told you four years ago that you really needed better bras. Your boobs were too low." She was right, I didn't remember. And the truth was, I was still wearing the same brand of bras. But I smiled and said, "Thank you." Because I'm pretty sure she meant to be supportive (ha-ha). And if not, I chose to take it that way anyway.

So I try never to take anything personally, and never to take myself too seriously. I mean, with a nickname like Gravity Gretchen, how could I? And knocking out my front teeth had a lot to do with that attitude too. Hard to get too full of yourself when you know that but for modern dentistry, you'd look like a snaggletoothed six-year-old.

I can't even tell you what a saga it's been with my teeth. I've had them done and redone numerous times, and every so often a crown pops off, which is not a glamorous look. Here's a photo one of my friends took in high school, if you need proof:

Glamour shot

When I was pregnant for the first time, my body rejected the implant my oral surgeon had put in. So, during that entire pregnancy, I had a "flipper"—front teeth on a retainer. I was in the House of Representatives at the time, and I'd sit in big caucus meetings and pop my teeth out, surprising colleagues, who'd look over and crack up. Most politicians would sooner crawl into a cave than be seen in public toothless, but I thought it was funny.

Gravity Gretchen has continued to make appearances throughout my political career. Toward the end of my first year as governor, a few of my old high school friends invited me to a tailgate in Ann Arbor before the Michigan–Michigan State game. I hadn't seen them in quite a while, and we were excited to reconnect. Of course, when you're governor, you don't just roll up in your own car to your friend's house. You have an official, unmarked SUV, a security detail of Michigan State Police officers, and sometimes a marked patrol car with lights and sirens as well.

So, we're a rolling show. As we pulled up to the house, everyone came out to see, and when I stepped out of the car, I slipped on the ice and fell right on my butt. My security detail tried to catch me, but no luck—I went sprawling on the pavement. You can protect me from other people, but you can't protect me from myself. Everyone burst out laughing, because this was absolutely on brand. Here comes the governor! Oh no, it's just Gravity Gretchen.

CHAPTER 6

RUN TOWARD THE FIRE

On May 25, 2020, George Floyd was murdered. A white police officer in Minneapolis knelt on his neck for more than nine minutes, ignoring Floyd's pleas to let up so he could breathe. I felt sick watching the video. And angry. Why were things like this still happening to members of our African American communities? When would we do the work to make sure every American felt safe and protected? Where was the sense of urgency to fix this appallingly broken component of our culture?

In the days after Floyd's death, I spoke as bluntly as I could about the systemic problems underlying this horrific incident. In brief remarks to reporters, I said:

> I cannot pretend that I understand the exhaustion
> or desperation that African Americans across our
> country are feeling right now. I can't imagine being
> a mother who's afraid every time her son goes out
> in public that he might not come home. But what

I do understand is that it's on every leader in this country to work urgently until we achieve that cultural change that's overdue.

George Floyd's death, and the deaths of many others—Ahmaud Arbery, Trayvon Martin, Renisha McBride—they're not isolated incidents. They're part of a systemic cycle of racial injustice in our country. . . . The events of the last couple of weeks have really sent a clear message that Black lives are under threat every single day.

In late May, thousands of people began protesting across Michigan. Emotions were running high, and although there were some clashes and a few curfews, the level of upheaval in our cities was less than in other parts of the country. Both of my daughters were deeply affected by the events of the summer and supportive of the Black Lives Matter movement, and Sydney was adamant that she wanted to join the protesters.

I had just lifted the stay-at-home order on June 1, as the number of new Covid cases was falling. Even so, I knew that if I went to a protest myself, I'd get heat for being in a crowd, masked or not. But seeing how my daughter's generation was taking the lead, and hearing Sydney talk about the importance of being there, helped me realize I needed to show up. There are times when our children become our consciences, reminding us that the only real failure is not trying.

On June 4, Lieutenant Governor Garlin Gilchrist, Colonel Joe Gasper of the Michigan State Police, and I joined with local faith leaders in a unity march through Detroit, organized by the Greater Grace Temple, to honor George Floyd's life and memory. As predicted, some did criticize me for choosing to march, calling my decision a "slap in the face" to Michiganders and claiming I hold myself to "a different standard than the rest of us." I don't, but it was an important moment to show support for the Black community. So I did.

Similarly, I have always tried to be an ally of LGBTQ+ people. And when my older daughter, Sherry, shared with me that she was a part of the community, it took on even greater weight. The fact that I had been a longtime supporter made it easier for her to understand and accept who she is, because she knew I was an ally.

"Part of the community" is also kind of an inside joke between my daughter Sherry and me after this text exchange. A good reminder that just because someone is younger than you, they still may have something to teach you. And they may also occasionally call you ridiculous.

We still have so much work to do, and it's decades overdue. We must never be afraid to show up.

On November 30, 2021, I got a call that a mass shooting was happening at Oxford High School, just north of Detroit, and an unknown number of people had been injured or killed.

I was in Detroit, and my first instinct was to go straight to Oxford, but my detail refused to take me into a dangerous situation that was still developing. State police are conditioned to run to the fire—except when they're assigned to the governor's detail. Their job is to keep me safe, and until we knew the situation was contained, they weren't taking me anywhere near that high school.

We found an office space with a television and watched as reports began trickling out from Oxford. At least three people were dead, with many more injured. A shooter had been subdued and arrested, but were there more? My phone kept buzzing with calls from officials in Oakland County, and we tried to figure out when it would be safe to go. It felt wrong that I had people working to keep me safe while children were in danger. I just felt compelled to be with the people of Oxford, to show them that we stood with them in this most horrific time of need.

As soon as we got the all clear, we rushed to the SUV and headed north. Sitting in the back, as we sped up the highway with lights flashing, I wasn't sure what I could say that might be helpful to this grieving, traumatized community. So I called

Dan Malloy, who was the governor of Connecticut when the Sandy Hook shootings happened, to ask for his advice. Dan and I had met a few times over the years, but I didn't know him well. I just laid it out: "I'm going to the scene of a shooting, and I have no idea what to say."

"Don't talk about yourself," he told me. "Just show up, and keep showing up. Be present. Don't jump into policy conversations about gun laws but focus on the community and healing." I thanked Dan and resolved to follow his advice.

Despite the freezing temperatures, the press briefing was held outside, across the street from the school. As I stepped out of the car, a member of my security detail lent me a jacket, and I took my place beside first responders as a representative from the Sheriff's Department stepped up to speak. He gave details of the shooting, saying that the gunman, a student at the school, had been apprehended and that three students had been killed, "a sixteen-year-old male, a fourteen-year-old female, and a seventeen-year-old female." Hearing those ages made me think of my own daughters, and I felt tears welling up for the parents, families, and community impacted by this violence. That was the moment he asked if I'd like to say a few words.

I stepped up to the microphone, feeling nervous and emotional. I thanked the first responders for their quick action, then said:

> My heart goes out to the families; this is an
> unimaginable tragedy. I hope that we can all rise

to the occasion and wrap our arms around the families, the affected children and school personnel, and this community. It is an unimaginable tragedy and just—I just wanted to be here because I think this is an important moment for us to support one another, to support this community, and I want to thank our first responders again.

That was all I said, and I felt lucky to have gotten through it without crying. But a few minutes later, during a short Q&A period, a reporter who could see that I was struggling said, "You're still deeply affected by this. Talk to us about that."

I looked at her, my throat tight. "I think this is every parent's worst nightmare," I said, my voice cracking at the end. It was all I could manage to say. I cannot begin to fathom the trauma felt by the students there that day. How can we expect students to be excited about learning when this tragedy plays out in American schools, and only American schools, again and again?

The people of Oxford understood that their pain was shared. And that was what mattered. We ultimately lost four promising young Michiganders in that shooting—Madisyn Baldwin, Tate Myre, Hana St. Juliana, and Justin Shilling, whose lives were cut far too short.

I've learned while doing this job in unprecedented times, you've got to go in, and you've got to do it fast. Because it's a rare problem that is self-solving; most get worse over time.

Showing support for the Black community after George Floyd, and being at Oxford after the shooting, helped give me clarity about what we needed to do to make our people safer. You're not going to get everything right immediately, but you've got to get in there and try.

Gun violence is the number one cause of death for children in America. This is a shocking statistic, especially because in most countries similar to ours, it doesn't even make the top four. Our nation's lax gun laws, plus the sheer number of firearms available, has led to a terrible situation where from a very young age, our kids have to prepare for the possibility of a mass shooting.

By now, nearly all Americans have had their lives touched by gun violence, but about fifteen months after the Oxford shooting, another shooting, at Michigan State University, brought to light a grim new milestone when students who had already survived one school shooting found themselves in the midst of another. Some had survived the Oxford High School shooting, and at least one student had been at Sandy Hook Elementary.

On the evening of Monday, February 13, a gunman opened fire on the campus of Michigan State University. He shot seven people in Berkey Hall, killing two, then walked down the street firing shots into other buildings. Students scrambled to hide or flee, while others stayed behind to take care of their wounded classmates. As heavy and horrible as active-shooter drills are, these kids knew what to do, and some ended up saving fellow students' lives.

Someone called 911 almost immediately, and what followed were an intense few hours while the gunman was still at large. I was at home, getting updates from the police, and at first it was unclear how many shooters there were, where they were, and how many people had been killed. The situation was chaotic.

Though neither of my daughters were students at MSU, both of them had friends on campus. That night, Sydney was in her apartment, glued to the news and texting with her friends to make sure they were okay. Sherry's best friend was at MSU, and though she wasn't near the shootings, she—like so many of the school's students—was deeply affected by the events of that night. It seemed like everyone in Michigan knew someone who was there, and together we mourned more of our children lost to gun violence. Three students lost their lives that day: Arielle Anderson, Brian Fraser, and Alexandria Verner.

The shootings at MSU galvanized students and their families. And because we had recently redrawn formerly gerrymandered districts and sworn in a new state legislature, we were able to pass bills for secure weapons storage, background checks, and extreme risk protection orders (red flag laws). Their work made the difference. The fight for gun safety has been hard, excruciating, and long. But it's worth having, because we shouldn't have to live like this. More important, our young people shouldn't have to grow up under the constant threat of gun violence in their classrooms, at a parade, at a concert, or anywhere. Period.

In 2012, just after the Sandy Hook shootings, Liz's then-nine-year-old daughter Maggie asked her, "What were school shootings like when you were a kid, Mom?" The question breaks my heart, because for generations, kids were able to go to school without fearing random shooters roaming the hallways. Every child deserves that.

It was students and their families who made a difference in Michigan, and you can too. We just have to keep pushing until we get back to a place of safety and sanity. It simply doesn't happen in any other country, and it shouldn't happen here, either.

CHAPTER 7

SEEK TO UNDERSTAND

I'm an early-to-bed kind of person, so I don't watch late-night shows. But when I woke up on Sunday, April 26, 2020, my phone was blowing up with people saying that *Saturday Night Live* had done a sketch about me. At the time, *SNL* was having cast members film themselves from home, and Cecily Strong had put on a straight-haired brown wig and some truly epic false eyelashes, then filmed herself talking about the pandemic out on a back porch with a bunch of trees behind her. "We're not out of the woods," she says, gesturing behind her. "We never will be! We live in Michigan."

When I first started watching the sketch I was worried. Were they going to make a joke of me? Was this going to be embarrassing? But soon I was laughing. Cecily's accent was definitely over the top, but she was portraying me as a rugged Michigan woman drinking beer and standing up to bullies. What's not to like? Referring to protesters who had been gathering at the capitol in Lansing, she said, "Stay home. I promise you can call me a bitch from the safety of your house. It's called Twitter!" She urged them to social distance, saying that "If the tip of your AK-47 can touch the tip of your buddy's AK? Back up!" And she told them to "wear face masks. But not a Joker mask. And not a clown mask. And absolutely no masks that come with a hood."

The sketch was funny, but it was inspired by scary developments in Michigan. About ten days earlier, raw anger about Covid stay-at-home orders had boiled over into an aggressive protest at the capitol. Unbeknownst to the protesters, I was nearby, watching it all in person. And for the first time, but unfortunately not the last, I felt afraid not just for my own safety, but for the safety of my family, staff, and others around me.

On Wednesday, April 15, 2020, I went to my office in the George W. Romney Building, across the street from the capitol. I was preparing for my regular Covid briefing in the press auditorium when we heard cars honking, people shouting, and bullhorns blaring. A group called the Michigan Conservative Coalition was staging an "Operation Gridlock" protest, and hundreds of cars and trucks had rolled downtown at noon with the goal of shutting down the streets.

Two days earlier, I'd told reporters that I had no problem with the planned protest, as long as people stayed in their cars or at a safe distance from one another, to limit the spread of the virus. I understood that people felt frustrated and angry, and this was a way they could make themselves heard. We live in a society where there's a full spectrum of different opinions.

While my goal is always to find common ground, it's not possible for everyone to get what they want. But the next best thing I can do is to let them know I'm listening. People have a right to feel the way they feel and to be acknowledged. And by listening, I can learn something.

So, when the honking and noise started up, I didn't mind. But when I went to look out the window, I was shocked at what I saw.

Swastikas. Confederate flags. AR-15s. And though I didn't see this until later, one man had tied a noose around the neck of a brown-haired Barbie doll, dangling her from a pole.

There were signs that read "Free Michigan, Impeach Whitmer," "All workers are essential," and "Rural lives matter." A blue van had a bumper sticker that read "Help destroy America!" But the ones that stopped me short were the big hand-lettered signs saying "Adolf Whitler is killing small businesses!" and "Heil Witmer!" It was bad enough being called a Nazi, but the next sign I saw was a threat: "HalfWhit is the reason we need the 2nd amendment." This was a reference to the Second Amendment to the Constitution, which guarantees the right to bear arms. In other words, the sign holder was expressing the opinion that I should be shot.

I'd been looking out the window for a couple of minutes, taking photos with my phone, but when I saw those signs, I took a step back. The legislature wasn't in session that day, so I doubted anyone realized I was there, and it suddenly felt important to keep it that way. I knew that people were angry, but the fury, hateful imagery, and overt threats of violence shocked me, especially since some had brought their kids to the protest.

Most people were in their vehicles, but others were milling around the capitol steps, and the only masks in sight were the face-covering headgear known as balaclavas—because even though the protesters refused to wear masks that would protect themselves and others from the virus, they were fine wearing masks to keep from being identified. That was the moment that I realized just how far apart we were during this pandemic. If we ever needed to pull together, now was the time. But it was becoming clear that the more I tried to put measures in place that would protect people, the more some would push back.

The view from my office window

During the demonstration, a couple of Michigan State Police troopers on my security detail went down to make sure no violence was about to break out with me in the area. As soon as I finished my briefing, I just wanted to go home. I felt incredibly discouraged, sad, and perplexed. Six weeks earlier, we didn't have a single reported case of Covid in our state. Now, so many people had died in such a short time that some morgues had to bring in refrigerated trucks to hold the bodies. Our hospitals were so overrun, they couldn't treat people with other life-threatening medical emergencies, because they didn't have the beds.

I was trying to keep people from dying, and this was the response? Swastikas and hanging me in effigy? I understood that I was asking the people of Michigan to make sacrifices while we navigated this crisis. What I didn't understand, and still don't, is the reaction that because I was trying to save lives, people were threatening mine.

I hoped that the protests would allow people to blow off steam and that the situation would settle down. Instead, a week later, a crowd of people armed with semiautomatic weapons showed up at our home. We live in the governor's residence, a ranch-style house that was built in the 1950s and donated to the state in 1969. Our street is quiet and friendly, and though the house is surrounded by a gate, it blends in to the rest of the neighborhood. It's low-key in true Michigan fashion, where we view conspicuous displays of wealth or power with a healthy side-eye.

On the morning of April 23, I was at home with my husband, Marc, Sherry and Sydney, and our dog, Kevin (we didn't yet have our other dog, Doug). Our security detail was there too, but they tend to stay out of sight, so when we first started hearing yelling, chanting, and music blaring outside, Marc and I just looked at each other like, *What the hell?* We peeked out a window, saw a couple dozen people outside the gate, then quickly closed the blinds again. Awakened by all the yelling, my daughters came out of their bedrooms, saying, "Mom, what's going on?"

"Protesters," I said. We wanted to see what was happening but didn't want to be seen, and the only window where we could do that was in the guest bathroom at the front of the house. So Marc, the girls, and I crowded into the bathroom (with Kevin) and peered out the window. We could see people with AR-15s, American flags, and MAGA signs, and there was a huge Trump float that had been appearing at rallies all over Michigan.

My girls are like me—pretty even-keeled and not easily thrown. But seeing people with semiautomatic weapons standing just outside our home was chilling for all of us. What did they want? I struggled to understand the depths of their anger. We were all in this together. Covid didn't discriminate based on party affiliation. We all felt nervous and kept the shades drawn for the rest of that day.

The crowd stayed for hours, yelling and chanting. When they finally left, I dared to hope that things would at last calm down. Unfortunately, once again, the opposite turned out to be true.

• • • •

Around this same time, a group of men calling themselves the Wolverine Watchmen began formulating a plan. A few months later, when fourteen men were arrested, this would be referred to as a "kidnapping plot." But the reality is some of the men discussed killing me. They weren't going to keep me tied up in a basement somewhere. They weren't going to ransom me. It was an apparent assassination plan.

In April, with most of the Covid restrictions still in place, the plotters began talking about taking violent action against government officials and law enforcement, engaging in firearms training, and running military tactical drills. Fortunately, one man who'd joined the group in early 2020, a decorated Iraq War veteran named Dan Chappel, was concerned enough that he reached out to law enforcement. He became an FBI informant, and much of what we know about the plot ultimately came from him.

On April 30, some of the plotters joined other heavily armed protesters at the capitol for an "American Patriot Rally." They flooded into the building—which the police allowed, since Michigan was one of nine states that allowed open carry of weapons in the state capitol.* They entered the upper gallery of

---

* In 2021, in response to these events, the Capitol Commission banned open carry of guns in the building. In 2023, it banned concealed carry for anyone except members of the legislature.

the Senate chamber, leading to a surreal scene of camouflaged, masked men armed with semiautomatic weapons hovering over the nervous legislators on the floor below.

I was working from home that day and only realized something was happening when my sister Liz called to see if I was okay. I turned on the news and was stunned to see images of armed, masked men standing outside the door of my office in the capitol. It was a surreal feeling.

The protesters were getting bolder, and the plotters ramped up their planning. The FBI embedded more informants in the group, and over the next few months they gathered hundreds of hours of recordings and videos, and thousands of text messages. The group talked about storming the state capitol, taking hostages, and executing them on live television. They discussed locking down the building from the outside while the legislature was in session, then setting it on fire.

At first, I didn't know anything about these plots. But early that summer, the head of my security detail, Michigan State Police lieutenant Scott McManus, asked to meet with me. We sat down in the sunroom of the governor's residence, and he said, "I need to let you know about a situation." He told me about the plan to kidnap and kill me and let me know that the FBI had an informant embedded in the group. "This is serious," he said, "but the FBI and the state police are working closely together. You are safe, and your family is safe."

I found all of this hard to process. I understood that the

stay-at-home orders were difficult and that they impacted people's livelihoods and financial situations. I got why people didn't like masking—I don't particularly like it either! Some people feel like they can't breathe well, and it can make your face sweat or break out. I had taken all this into consideration, but ultimately the good that these steps did was worth the inconveniences they caused.

There was no one-size-fits-all fix for the pandemic. And there was irony in the fact that the people protesting the stay-at-home orders most loudly were doing it in public, unmasked, wherever and whenever they wanted.

What was I missing? I genuinely wanted to understand how people had gotten angry enough to actually want to kill me. But for the moment, I needed to focus not on the feelings of those who would harm me, but on my family. While I was upset at learning of the plot, it wasn't because I was especially worried about my safety. I trusted my security detail to protect me. But I knew that this information could have a big impact on my now-teenaged daughters, and I wanted to try to minimize the fear they might feel.

I told the girls in the kitchen one afternoon. They remember that I said it nonchalantly, just dropping in the conversational tidbit that "Oh, just so you know—there's a plot to kidnap and kill me, but it's never going to happen, so don't worry about it!" Fortunately, this tactic worked well; because I didn't seem worried, they didn't worry either. Sherry and Sydney are stoic

Whitmers, and amid all the chaos of 2020, it probably felt like just one more crazy event.

We carried on with our lives, trying not to think about whatever threats might be looming outside our four walls. Meanwhile, the plotters were becoming more brazen. In July, the men began training to storm a house and capture people inside. They built a replica, calling it a "kill house," and practiced taking hostages. That same month, one was recorded saying "Snatch and grab, man. Grab the fuckin' governor. Just grab the bitch. Because at that point, we do that, dude—it's over." In August, another texted "Have one person go to her house. Knock on the door and when she answers it just cap her."

In August, Scott asked to meet with me again. He told me that the FBI had learned that the plotters were doing reconnaissance on a small cottage Marc and I had bought years before in Elk Rapids. And that's when things got really scary. While the governor's residence in Lansing felt extremely secure, our cottage was near the road, a small, one-story private residence with no gate. If I happened to be there when armed people showed up wanting to kidnap or hurt me, I would be vulnerable.

I wasn't there, thank goodness. But Marc was.

At the beginning of the summer, we weren't really traveling, because of Covid. As the summer wore on, and we relaxed the restrictions, Marc had started going up to the cottage occasionally. And now he just happened to be there on a weekend when the plotters were headed that way. I called him and said,

"You've got to leave"—which he did, very quickly. The plotters scoped out not only our cottage, but a nearby bridge, which they discussed blowing up to slow police response.

This was all way too close for comfort. My daughters initially hadn't been worried, but when we told them that the men had actually been skulking around our cottage, they got scared. To this day, neither Sherry nor Sydney has gone back there, even though it was always one of our favorite places to go as a family.

When the plotters met to discuss buying explosives from an undercover informant, the FBI finally had the evidence it needed. In early October, federal and state police officials arrested thirteen men. Another was arrested a week later. Though they refer to themselves as being in "militias," I prefer to call them what they are: domestic terrorists. Because these Michigan "militias" are the same groups that helped train Timothy McVeigh and Terry Nichols, who murdered 168 people when they bombed the Alfred P. Murrah Federal Building in Oklahoma City in 1995.

The day after the arrests, I gave a statement from my ceremonial office in the capitol. While I came down hard on the perpetrators, as well as the president, who continued "stoking distrust, fomenting anger, and giving comfort to those who spread fear and hatred and division," I also made a point of acknowledging how difficult the pandemic had been for everyone:

> 2020 has been a hard year for all of us. Hard for
> our doctors and nurses, and truck drivers, and

grocery store workers. It's been hard for the
teachers and students and parents, hard for those
who have had to stay isolated to stay safe. I get it,
life has been hard for us all. . . .

I think about all the moms who are working from
home, making breakfast every day, logging their kids
onto their Zoom class, and doing the laundry. I think
about the small-business owners who spent a lifetime
building something great, who are now hanging on
by their fingernails just to keep the lights on.

I wasn't saying all this to score political points. When I
signed those executive orders, it affected my own family's lives
too. When my daughters were born, I remember thinking, *How
cool—they'll be in the class of 2020 and the class of 2021, what
great years!* And then those turned out to be the worst possible years for any young person. With a stroke of my pen, I
had canceled my own kid's high school graduation, her senior
prom—all the stuff that other people were mad about. *Believe
me,* I wanted to scream, *I get it!*

Just as I had spent time seeking to understand, I wanted to
ask the people of my state to seek to understand me, too. So I
closed with a request:

Make no mistake, there will be more hard days
ahead. But I want the people of Michigan to know

this. As your governor, I will never stop doing everything in my power to keep you and your family safe. You don't have to agree with me, but I do ask one thing. Never forget that we are all in this together. Let's show a little kindness and a lot more empathy. Let's give one another a little grace, and let's take care of each other. . . . I know we can get through this. We will get through this. So let's get through it together.

You might be curious as to why, in the face of all this difficulty and stress, I decided to run for reelection two years later. When I was gearing up for that campaign, I did have moments of wondering whether it made sense to keep putting not just myself, but my family and colleagues through all of this. I reached out to a few colleagues, in particular other Democratic women governors, to talk it through. And in the end, I felt like I had to run, and had to win, to show those who would threaten me that most people believed in the measures we were taking. When I won that second election by a larger margin than the first, I felt vindicated and even more confident in the direction we were heading.

Nearly three years down the road, there's no doubt that the apparent kidnapping and murder plot changed me.

I've always loved meeting people and mingling in big groups.

But now, when I walk into a party or event, I find myself scanning the room. I look for anything that seems off and take note of where the doors are. It's not that I live in fear, but there's a heightened awareness now that I didn't have before. Not just as a governor, but as a person. As a mom, and as a wife.

Marc had to close his dental practice due to threats. He'd shut it temporarily when the pandemic began and had been happy to reopen. Unfortunately, the threatening calls kept coming, and it just didn't seem safe for him, his patients, or his employees to keep going. He lost his job, and his patients lost their trusted dentist.

In 2021, I took Sherry to the Traverse City Cherry Festival on a campaign swing. We had a nice day planned, with a parade and festival, and starting with a visit to a local store for some chocolate-covered cherries. Before we walked in, my detail went first in civilian clothes to scope it out. They took note of a couple of armed men in the crowd, and when I walked in the door, one of them said, "There's that bitch." The detail came to me and said, "Governor, we're leaving." We hustled out the back door and into the SUV, which immediately sped off. When they told me why, I was crushed. And angry.

The most maddening moment, though, came in April of 2022. I had gone to opening day at Comerica Park to see the Tigers, a fun tradition for every governor. I walked around the stadium, stopping and saying hello to people, shaking hands and posing for photos. I was having a blast, when suddenly my chief of staff, JoAnne Huls, took my arm and whispered, "The verdict is in."

Though a few of the plotters had pleaded guilty, the first of several trials had recently gone to the jury. Four men were charged with conspiring to commit kidnapping, and the evidence against them was strong. One was the man who'd said "Knock on the door and when she answers it just cap her." Another had been recorded saying "If this whole thing starts to happen, I'm telling you what, dude, I'm taking out as many of those motherfuckers as I can. Every single one."

JoAnne found us a small office in the stadium where we could listen to the verdict, and I figured we'd be, if not celebrating, at least feeling a measure of relief. We put my legal counsel, Mark Totten, on speakerphone, and as he read aloud the verdict, my heart sank. The two men who'd made the statements above were acquitted. The other two had a hung jury, meaning the jury was unable to decide whether or not they were guilty.*

I felt gutted. How had this happened? There was so much evidence, so many recordings and texts and months of plotting. So much work by the FBI and state police. And now these guys

---

* Ultimately, thanks to the great work of Attorney General Dana Nessel and her team, and the federal prosecutors, eight out of the fourteen who were indicted ended up in prison, including the two who had a hung jury that day. One other person received probation.

were going to walk free? Even JoAnne, one of the most unflappable people I know, was in shock. We left the game, feeling depressed nearly to the brink of despair.

On that day, I let myself feel the frustration and disappointment. But as soon as I was able to move past the shock, I became determined, once again, to understand. Or at the very least, to try.

I asked whether I could meet with one of the handful of plotters who'd pleaded guilty and taken responsibility for their actions, just to talk. Mark checked with our attorney general, Dana Nessel, who said it might be possible. With all the various trials and appeals, the time isn't yet right. But I do look forward to being able to sit and talk, face-to-face. To ask the questions and really hear the answers. And hopefully to take some small step toward understanding.

A NOTE ON GRATITUDE

Years ago, I started keeping what I call my gratitude journal. I don't write very much, but at the end of each day, I jot down three or four things for which I'm grateful.

Some days in our lives are more difficult than others, and it can be hard to focus on the positive. But there's never been a day when I couldn't come up with at least three items. And I'm here to tell you, the difficult days are the ones when writing what I'm grateful for feels the most helpful.

Our dogs, Kevin and Doug, make frequent appearances in the journal.

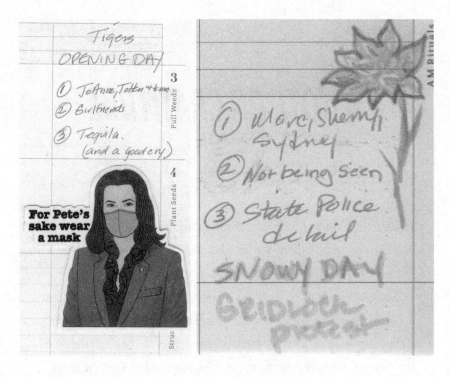

(Left) The day a jury acquitted two plotters.
(Right) From the day of the gridlock protest. I was grateful
no one saw me in my office window.

CHAPTER 8

YOU'LL NEVER REGRET BEING KIND

In late November of 2019, I was meeting with business leaders while on a trade mission to Israel when my cell phone pinged with a strange text message. It was from our State Senate majority leader, Republican Mike Shirkey.

"Gretchen," he wrote, "I'm sure you're not hearing this from me first. I was in what I presumed was a very private meeting. A little 'too loose' with my conversation. Said some things disrespectful but not intended to be personal."

Umm . . . okay. This was actually the first I was hearing about it—whatever it was. I could only imagine what Shirkey might have said, but it must have been bad if he was texting me privately to apologize. Although, as it turned out, he wasn't apologizing but suggesting he'd like to sometime in the future. "So, just know I'm not totally clueless," he went on. "Should not have taken those liberties. I own it. And I hope I have a chance to personally apologize to you when you return. Very sorry if it offends you. Mike."

I asked JoAnne to find out what I may or may not be offended by, and soon we had our answer. During a meeting with young Republicans at Hillsdale College, a private Christian school, Shirkey had said that negotiating with me was difficult, because I was "on the batshit-crazy spectrum." It's not an especially Christian thing to say, obviously, not to mention being a slur on anyone who is neurodivergent or suffers from mental illness. It was offensive on many levels, and not helpful at a time when we were trying to work together after disagreeing over the state budget.

Shirkey and I were far apart politically, and he was known for speaking his mind in colorful and occasionally offensive ways. In 2008, he called then-candidate Barack Obama a "clown," saying that anyone thinking of voting for him should "test the Kool-Aid they are drinking." In 2014, he opposed a local ordinance prohibiting discrimination against LGBTQ+ people, calling it "dangerous." Years later, he would challenge me to a fistfight on the capitol lawn, brag that he "spanked" me on legislation, claim that the January 6 insurrection was a "hoax," and, worst of all, he would be pictured in public with one of the men who was charged in the 2020 plot.

Unlike lawmakers, governors don't have the luxury of base-baiting, hurling insults, or stepping into the Octagon with those in the opposing party.* My professional relationship with

---

* An Ultimate Fighting Championship reference, for those of you who aren't fight fans.

Shirkey was not ideal, to say the least. But I needed to be able to work with him moving forward, so I thought carefully about how to respond.

It felt important to address the insult that he'd felt free to express behind closed doors. "I'm sad to see the kind of rhetoric that's been used," I told reporters. "I think that does a disservice to our ability to find some common ground . . . I ran against that, and I'm not going to return it in kind." That was all I said about it.

Two weeks later, though, I decided to revisit the "batshit" incident once more. Shirkey was about to celebrate his sixty-fifth birthday, so I arranged to send him a yellow layer cake with black frosting, decorated on top with a bat and the words "Happy 65th BAT Day!" This was meant as a little private joke, a way to defuse any lingering tension. To my surprise, Shirkey posted a photo of the cake on X/Twitter, with the message "Having a 'batiful' birthday thanks to my friend @GovWhitmer." I replied with a tweet saying, "Hope your day isn't too 'crazy' 🦇."

It would have been easy—and no doubt satisfying!—for me to fire back at Shirkey. But as tempting as it was to clap back, we needed to put the incident behind us. I couldn't afford to have open warfare with the Senate majority leader—we had too much to do for the people of Michigan.

If there's any one motto I live by in my political career, it's "get shit done"—even if that means gritting your teeth and putting on a smile when you really feel like punching a throat. Once a situation escalates, it can easily spiral out of control. That's why I try to follow my dad's "twenty-four-hour rule." He never reacted to anything emotionally but always said that if you're still angry twenty-four hours after something happened, then it's time to figure out a response.

Once, when I was in high school, I snuck out of the house in the middle of the night with a friend who was staying over. We left the back door unlocked so we could sneak back in—clever, right? Unfortunately, when we got back to the house, it was locked, and all the lights were on. We sheepishly rang the bell, and the door swung open to reveal my very unhappy father. He didn't say a word that night, which was somehow even worse than getting yelled at. He didn't say anything until the next day, while I twisted miserably in the wind. When he finally sat me down with his yellow pad and an outline and talked calmly about how disappointed he was in my behavior, it was a whole lot more effective than if he'd just started yelling at me the night before.

We've all had times where we blurt out something in anger or fire off a hurtful message to someone, then realize the next day that we've done damage we can't take back. You'll never regret taking a moment and responding with kindness, as hard as it may be to do. I learned this lesson way back in 2000, during my first political campaign.

• • • •

After graduating from law school, I had taken a job with Dickinson Wright, a multinational firm founded in Michigan in 1878. This was a plum job for a new lawyer, and I was proud to have gotten it. But while I loved my colleagues, I quickly grew discontented with the job itself. My days were spent sitting in a law library, writing multipage legal briefs, with little interaction with the outside world.

Two years in, I was about to tear my hair out. Then, out of the blue, a politically connected friend of mine called. "Your state representative can't run again because of term limits," he told me. "We don't have a candidate in your district, so you should think about running."

I had never considered running for political office, even though I had enjoyed my internship with state representative Curtis Hertel, my early mentor. Hertel was a tough guy, but also kind and friendly. By watching his example, I had learned how to disagree without being disagreeable. He never took anything personally, and he took seriously his job of being an advocate for his people.

So I really liked working for him, and after graduating from college I went back to his office for a year before starting law school. This was my first "real" full-time job. I didn't make a lot of money, but spending my days around interesting and inspiring people made up for that. This was my entry into adulthood, including my first time living alone. I rented an apartment and decorated it how I liked it, not having to worry about anyone else's opinion. There was something freeing in knowing that if the kitchen was a mess, it was *my* mess.

When I finished law school and passed the bar, I moved naturally into practicing law. But when I heard about this opportunity to run for an open seat in the State House, it got me thinking. I ran the idea past each of my parents (separately, because they'd been divorced for years by then), and they both encouraged me to jump in. That's when I got excited. At age twenty-eight, I announced my candidacy.

All my campaigns have been family affairs, starting with that very first one. My parents both got actively involved, going door-knocking with me and coming down to my little campaign headquarters to help with mailings. Mom would bring homemade sandwiches for all the volunteers, barking "Eat a damn vegetable!" and cracking us all up. We spent long hours stuffing envelopes, but somehow she managed to make it fun.

It was exhilarating to be out on the campaign trail. Even though I was in motion from morning to night, I never felt tired at the end of the day. Like a lot of people who end up going into politics, I discovered that meeting and talking with people, even for hours on end, gave me energy.

At this point, there were three other candidates in the Democratic primary for the open seat. And a few weeks from the August primary election, I was down by about twenty points to one of them—Mary Lindemann, who as the wife of a long-serving elected public works official named Pat Lindemann was considered by many to be the heir apparent to the seat. There's a common misconception that people who are related to office-holders are somehow more entitled to hold office themselves. In these cases, I think about something Representative Eric Swalwell once said: "My position has always been that the House of Representatives does not take reservations. It's walk-in only."

By this point in my campaign, we needed a game-changer, or there was no way I was going to win. I called a meeting with my staff, and my parents came too. One campaign adviser was adamant that it was time to go after my opponent. "We've got to go scorched-earth," he said. "It's our only chance." I didn't feel comfortable with this idea—but I also didn't want to lose. Before I could comment or ask questions, though, my dad spoke up.

"Gretchen," he said, "you are going to live in this community for a long time. If you go negative, win or lose, you will pay a price for it. You won't be proud of it." For a moment, everyone was silent. Then he turned to my staff and said, "What would it take to stay positive and win?"

"I don't think we can," the adviser replied. It's not that he relished the idea of going negative, but he couldn't see a clear path to victory otherwise.

Dad was unfazed. "What if we do everything we possibly can, bring absolutely everything to the table. What's our best option?"

After some discussion, we decided that our only real hope of staying positive and winning would be to ask former Michigan attorney general Frank J. Kelley to help. Frank was a state legend. He had served ten consecutive terms as AG—getting appointed at age thirty-six as the youngest in Michigan history and retiring at age seventy-four as the oldest. He was respected and admired by people of every political persuasion, and a national voice on justice, environmental issues, and consumer protection.

My mother had served as an assistant attorney general under Frank, and he was good friends with both my parents. So we decided to ask if he'd be willing to tape a campaign spot for me. If he agreed, we'd buy every minute of TV time we could find and hope that might be enough to squeak out a win. It would cost us three times as much to do this, and it still might not work. But Frank said yes, and we decided to do it.

We'll never know exactly how many votes Frank's support brought me, but it turned out to be enough. On primary day, I won the nomination by just 281 votes out of 5,133 cast—and for years after, people told me they'd voted for me because of Frank's endorsement. Now it was on to the general election, to try to win my first political seat.

I love this story, not only because it speaks to the power of a positive campaign, but because Frank J. Kelley was a symbol of positive governance. In his thirty-seven years as AG, Frank worked with many Republican governors, always telling them, "The people elected both of us, and they're counting on us to work together." That's a belief I share—and it's the reason I'd rather send someone a bat cake than flip them the bird, no matter how irritated I might be.

Frank's position was that we should try to see the humanity in one another—to recognize that we may have different values, but we're people with similar jobs. It wasn't all that long ago when legislators from different parties could grab a drink or a meal together, to talk about the issues of the day or even just catch up on each other's lives. These were the times when Democrats and Republicans could disagree without worrying that someone might show up with guns on their front lawn. There's deep division and mistrust between the parties today. But it hasn't always been like this, and it doesn't have to continue to be.

A big part of staying positive is realizing what's truly important and what to let go. In late 2000, just as I was on the brink of winning that first race, I found out in the hardest way imaginable where that line was.

With only a few weeks to go until election day, our campaign was firing on all cylinders. The best part of campaigning is getting to spend time with your family and friends who are supporting you, and I had particularly loved spending hours with my mom and dad during all those months of campaigning.

Soon, I would be even more grateful for all those hours.

My mother hadn't been feeling well, suffering from headaches she thought might be caused by an inner-ear infection. She'd been coming around the campaign office less often, but with the campaign in the home stretch, I had assumed she was just busy. (I've never known anyone who worked as hard as she did.) Then, with just days to go before the election, she got the devastating diagnosis of glioblastoma multiforme—the worst kind of brain cancer. *What? How could this be? What does it mean?* Mom was only fifty-eight and had always been in excellent health. Her diagnosis was shocking and traumatic, instantly pushing any thoughts of the campaign—or anything else—far into the background.

Within days, Mom went in for emergency surgery to remove as much of the tumor as they could and ease the pressure inside her skull. As I sat nervously with Liz, Richard, and our stepfather Don in the waiting room, my mom's boss, Attorney General (and future governor) Jennifer Granholm came to show her support. We sat there, mostly quiet, watching a TV affixed to the wall. And that's when an attack ad against me happened to pop up on the screen. My opponent was the chairman of the board of E. W. Sparrow Hospital, where my mother was being treated, and he had filmed the ad just a few floors above where I was now sitting. It was surreal to be watching him run me down for being the daughter of an insurance company executive, even as I sat right there in his hospital to await news of my mother's surgery.

If I had seen that ad before Mom's diagnosis, I would undoubtedly have been angry and upset. But only one thing mattered to me in that moment: what was happening with my mom in the operating room. I never have forgotten the valuable lesson I took from that day, that sometimes, events that seem so big and terrible and upsetting at the time are just . . . noise. If you can let go of a slight or an insult, then do. You'll be freeing yourself to focus on the things that genuinely matter.

The next two years brought some of the hardest moments of my life. Because Liz was living out of state, and I was the eldest sibling and always the caretaker among us, I took the primary role in caring for our dying mother. At the same time, I was also taking care of my newborn first daughter, Sherry, who was named after my mom. And I was serving as a freshman legislator, trying to learn the ropes in Lansing even as I spent my "free time" fighting with Mom's health insurance company, pumping breast milk, and changing diapers. Oh, yes—and my then-husband and I also moved into a new home. They say that five of the most stressful events in life are getting married, having a child, moving, starting a new job, and going through the death of a loved one. In that two-year period, I hit them all.

On June 4, 2002, my mom died. She was just fifty-nine years old, still cracking jokes and with a twinkle in her eye close to the end. I'm grateful to her for so many things: For raising my brother and sister and me to become the adults we are today. For leading by example, as a strong woman who took no crap and changed for no one. And for helping me to see, through both words and example, what really matters in life. I miss her every single day.

• • • •

There's one more reason why choosing to behave with kindness matters. Because it spreads.

In mid-May of 2020, it felt like the wheels were coming off the wagon. The pandemic was in full swing, with more than 47,000 Michiganders infected with Covid and more than 4,500 dead. People were still angry about the stay-at-home orders, and our economy was suffering. Eighteen months into my first term as governor, I was struggling to deal with a cascade of disasters that showed no signs of letting up.

And then, the dam broke. Literally.

After several days of heavy rain, including a massive downpour in the Midland area over May 17–18, the water levels in that area were rising to dangerous levels. The ninety-six-year-old Edenville Dam began showing ominous signs of stress, and on May 19, around six p.m., the earthen dike beside it gave way.

As sod and grass broke free, creating a small landslide, water from Wixom Lake burst through and rushed in a huge cascade toward Midland. Along the way, it overwhelmed a second dam, and now there was nothing holding back the water from flooding Midland and the surrounding villages. The Tittabawassee River, normally controlled by these two dams, rose a terrifying thirty-four feet as the wall of water surged toward people's homes, businesses, churches, schools, and anything else in the way.

Some people had evacuated after earlier warnings, but now

it was a matter of life and death to get others out safely. At ten p.m., I gave a press conference to issue an emergency declaration and urge people to "get somewhere safe now." I tried to project strength in the face of this calamity, but privately, I was shaken.

How much more can we take? I thought. In the middle of the night—in the middle of a pandemic!—people were having to evacuate their homes. How were we going to keep people safe, crammed into communal shelters? And what were we going to do with people who were sick or showing symptoms of Covid? How many once-in-a-lifetime disasters do we have to deal with at the same time?

As the flood bore down on Midland, ten thousand people were displaced from their homes. Some returned to their neighborhoods later to find their houses had been destroyed. Bridges were swept away, and the sewage system overwhelmed.

The next day, I went to Midland to survey the damage—the first time I'd left Lansing since the pandemic began. Michigan State Police took me up in a helicopter, and I had never seen anything like the scene below. It looked like a war zone, with vehicles strewn about, houses crushed, and mud and debris everywhere you looked. I felt so depressed, and so helpless. How were we going to get through this?

But then, back on the ground, I began talking with people in these devastated areas. I saw how neighbors were pitching in to help one another out. I watched as people showed up with mountains of casseroles and bags of groceries. I saw a community rising, coming together in the midst of a catastrophe to care for one another, regardless of what anyone's politics were. And for the first time in forty-eight hours, I felt hope.

At Midland High School, I spoke briefly with the press, to give an update on the situation. "I feel like I've said this a lot over the last ten weeks, but this is an event unlike anything we've seen before," I said. I described seeing the incredible devastation from the air, but instead of lingering on that, I turned to the moments of hope I'd seen. "I want to thank all of these people for all of their hard work, and these incredible volunteers who have brought food and supplies to help their fellow residents."

"We are gonna get through this," I continued. "We know that tough times don't last, but tough people do. We have seen a community come together, and we are going to continue to do that until we get through this crisis."

When something bad happens, it's natural to want to pull the covers over your head and ignore what's going on. But as the great folk singer Joan Baez says, "Action is the antidote to despair." I know that when I disengage, I feel worse, and when I'm out and about trying to make things happen, I feel better. Every person can make a difference, and the acts of kindness I saw from so many Michiganders that day really renewed my faith.

DON'T BURN YOUR BRIDGES

There's a really talented photographer who works a lot of the big political events in Michigan. He's been doing it for decades, starting when Governor James Blanchard was elected way back in 1983. And he not only takes great photos, he's also very chill and easy to work with, so I asked if he would be willing to shoot my 2018 campaign. I was thrilled he agreed to help, because everyone on my team knows and loves the guy. And, oh yeah—he also happens to be my ex-husband.

Divorce is never easy, but when Gary and I split up in 2008, we made a point of staying friendly, in part for the sake of our daughters, but also because it made all our lives simpler. Whitmers don't tend to hold grudges. As I've said, we have thick skin and short memories, which helps us to focus on what's happening now rather than what's happened in the past. I even thanked Gary and his new wife Alisande in my victory speech that year, which surprised people who didn't know us very well.

I try to do the same in my political life. Remember the

Republican Senate majority leader Randy Richardville, who I clashed with while trying to get the anti-bullying bill passed in 2011? We were far apart on many issues, but we worked to maintain a good relationship in spite of that. Four years after the anti-bullying episode, he told reporters he'd like to serve as my lieutenant governor on a bipartisan ticket if I ran for governor in 2018.

Another political opponent, Bob McCann, ran against me in my very first primary in 2000. Even though we were trying to beat each other, we maintained a friendly and supportive relationship, and he later came to work for me as communications director. In fact, he was the male staffer with me in the caucus room on the day in 2013 when I revealed my assault.

It's not always possible to keep good relations with people. Particularly these days, when political rhetoric often feels intensely personal and cruel, it can seem impossible to break through. But I believe it's worth trying, as long as you feel safe. You can always step away if a relationship feels truly toxic. The choice is yours.

In the case of maintaining good relations with my ex, it's been especially worth it for the gorgeous and sometimes goofy photos he's taken over the years. He takes our family photo every year . . . and whenever we see each other out at some event, we make sure to get a quick selfie and send it to our girls, who think we're goofballs.

*Our Brady Bunch–style blended family: Marc and me in front
(with dogs Kevin and Doug), and, behind us, Winston, Alex,
Sherry, Sydney, Hannah, and Mason.*

Photobomb!

Best ex-husband ever

CHAPTER 9

OWN YOUR SCREWUPS, AND FORGIVE OTHERS THEIRS

When I was about five years old, my mom took my best friend and me with her to run an errand at the drugstore. Walking to the car afterward, Mom noticed that our pockets were stuffed with candy. Little thieves! She marched the two of us right back into the store, told the clerk what we'd done, and instructed us to apologize. "Oh, it's okay," the clerk started to say, probably feeling bad for the two scared little shoplifters with the guilty looks on our faces.

"It is not okay!" my mom shouted. "You need to read them the riot act. And girls, you need to say you're sorry." The clerk halfheartedly reamed us out, and we sheepishly apologized. I never forgot how strongly Mom reacted that day, and how determined she was not only to make us return the candy but to say we were sorry for taking it.

When you screw up, you should own it. Yet for whatever reason, a lot of people don't like apologizing.

Maybe it feels like an uncomfortable admission of guilt.

In politics, people get advised all the time not to say they're sorry, but instead to use more squirrelly language to keep away the taint of blame. In America today, there's a perception that saying you're sorry makes you seem weak. But real strength is being able to recognize that we're all flawed. It's standing up, owning our mistakes, and taking the time to learn from them.

If you ask me, saying "I'm sorry" is a superpower. Those two tiny words can disarm angry people, make problems disappear, and heal rifts between friends. Saying you're sorry is a way of extending your hand across whatever divide separates you from another person, a way of opening yourself up and showing you care. And the best part is that it enables everyone to feel respected and heard and then move on.

In 2001, I got married for the first time. I was never a girl who dreamed of a big wedding, but what I did want was to have my mother there, and we were already on borrowed time. So we quickly arranged a small ceremony, followed by an intimate dinner.

The only nonfamily members I invited were Michelle, one of my closest friends since fifth grade, and Renee, the friend who'd introduced Gary and me. I just didn't have the bandwidth to do more. Another dear friend, Angie, was very hurt that she hadn't been included, particularly since I had been one of her bridesmaids. When I saw her at Michelle's wedding later that year, I thought she was frosty toward me—and I was crushed. Angie had been one of my very best friends since our freshman year of college, but in the midst of the terrible year I was having, I overreacted to what felt like a slight. With both of us feeling hurt, we didn't speak for over seven years.

In May 2008, I had a political event in Southern California and decided to invite both Angie and Michelle to join me. Angie is the kind of person who shows up for other people, and I was thrilled that she did that day. I had missed her and was so glad to know she wanted to reconnect too. She apologized for how she had behaved toward me. And after listening, I realized I owed her an apology too. With everything that had been going on, I hadn't been open and clear about the wedding and the limitations I was struggling with to make it happen, and neither one of us had communicated our feelings very well after that.

After we each apologized, we cried and drank and talked all night, and we've been like sisters ever since. In fact, in both 2018 and 2022, she moved to Michigan for a month to help me out in the home stretches of campaigns—cooking, charming folks all over the state, telling hilarious stories, and helping to keep me sane. When the time came, she helped me move from my house into the governor's residence. I couldn't even get my family to help with that! Rekindling our friendship after the rift was an absolute gift, and I can't tell you how much I regret those years we missed out on. But I'm incredibly grateful that we had enough sense to apologize to each other and revive a friendship we both treasure.

• • • •

In 2002, as my mom's cancer progressed, we had a wonderful hospice care team. They'd come and talk with us, make sure Mom was as comfortable as possible, and sometimes give us materials to read to help us get through that terrible time. I remain so grateful for the hospice workers, truly wonderful people who just want to help others through some of the worst days of their lives.

I remember being at my mom's place one day, just a month after I'd given birth. I put baby Sherry down in a laundry basket to sleep, picked up a pamphlet the hospice care worker had left, and read a story about a man riding on a subway train with six kids, all of whom were running wild and irritating everyone in the vicinity. A woman on the train decided she'd had enough and was about to give the man a piece of her mind. But as she opened her mouth to speak, he suddenly said, "My wife just died, and I don't know how I'm going to raise these kids on my own." And in that moment, everything changed for her, because she saw his humanity. Imagine how different the world would look right now if we could resist the urge to rush to judgment before trying to understand.

Even more than twenty years later, I still think of that story. We just never know what other people are going through. So, in the words of Ted Lasso, my favorite TV character, it's best to

"Be curious, not judgmental." (Unfortunately, he misattributes this quote to Walt Whitman, but nobody's perfect, not even Ted Lasso. Although he's close.)*

There have been times when I've found myself acting like the irritated woman in the pamphlet. During my time in the Senate, I didn't have a great relationship with the Republican chair of a committee on which I was serving. When she made the unusual move of instructing members to travel around the state for meetings, rather than holding them in Lansing, I was irritated. I had two small children, and now I'd have to make special arrangements for them so I could go on an unnecessary road show. When she didn't turn up for a scheduled stop in Grand Rapids, I was supremely annoyed.

"Well," I announced at the meeting, "it would've been nice if the chairwoman had made it."

And then I was informed that she couldn't come because her husband was in the hospital.

Oof. I felt like such a jerk. I was ashamed of my behavior and apologized to her both publicly and privately. She accepted it, and although that theoretically put an end to the matter, I still feel bad to this day that I made that comment. But the interesting outcome was that from then on, the tone

---

* So who said it? The phrase first appeared in a 1986 advice column by Marguerite and Marshall Shearer. Can't blame the *Ted Lasso* writers for not using that.

between us was more collegial. My act of apologizing, and hers of accepting it, had a lasting positive effect.

During my second term in the House, I began gaining my footing after a rough two years of caring for my mom and my newborn at the same time—the classic "sandwich-generation" situation, when a person has to take care of family members who are both younger and older than herself. I had spent my first term learning the ropes and listening, and then, after getting reelected, I began to take a more active role in party strategy and planning. I put together the team that won the Democratic leadership race, and when my slate won, I was appointed to the top position on appropriations for the Democrats.

Legislatures run on a pretty rigid set of rules and protocols, and when the minority leader officially announced that I'd be the top person on appropriations, it rankled the Republican Speaker of the House, who'd usually be the one to make that announcement. The Republicans got fired up about it, threatening to block me from the position. And that's when I realized that, even though I hadn't done anything wrong, I was the one who could, and should, fix the problem. To do the job I had been elected to do, it was on me to address it.

I bought a basket of goodies from a local bakery, including a nice bottle of olive oil, and presented it to the Republican chair of the appropriations committee. This was my "olive branch," a way of saying I was sorry we hadn't followed protocol and

asking if we could smooth things over. And that was all it took—
the Republicans stood down. I could have refused to apologize,
because I hadn't done anything wrong. But I've learned over
the years that it's better to focus on being effective than on
winning an argument.

During my first campaign for the House, I was out knocking on doors one blazing hot August afternoon, trying to close
the gap between me and the front-runner, Mary Lindemann,
before the primary vote later that month. Suddenly my campaign manager, Dan Curran, came flying around the corner in
his old brown four-door sedan you could hear coming from
a mile away. He screeched to a stop, rolled down his window,
and yelled, "Get in the car! Get in the car!"

"Thank you very much! I'd appreciate your support! Gotta
go!" I said to the person I'd been speaking with, then turned
and sprinted to the car. I shoved the campaign literature and
empty coffee cups out of the passenger seat, and as Dan tore off,
tires squealing, I said, "What is going on?"

"I screwed up!" he said, panic in his voice. "The debate is not
tomorrow—it's right now! We've got to get to WKAR. They're
waiting for us!"

This was . . . not ideal. Being punctual is a Whitmer family
trait, and I tend to arrive early for appointments—especially
important ones like this. I was sweating and red-faced, not at
all put together like I normally would be for a debate. I didn't
have a fresh change of clothes, no makeup, nothing. I wanted

to kill Dan, but he felt so terrible that I couldn't stay mad. I'd just have to roll with the situation and do the best I could.

When we got to the studio, I rushed in and took my place with the other candidates. Mary Lindemann was giving me a look similar to the one on my mom's face all those years ago when she marched me back into the drugstore to admit my crimes. Mary seemed to think that I was trying to play some kind of head game. Who shows up a half hour late for a debate, in the final days of a close race? She seemed furious, coming at me hard throughout the debate while I tried to stay composed, at the same time trying to hide the fact that I'd sweated through my shirt.

After it was over, I went immediately over to her. "Mary," I said, "I am so sorry." I explained what had happened, and it was like I'd flipped a switch. She'd been so wound up, so angry and defensive, and I could see her physically relax. Even though it wasn't my fault that I got there so late, the buck stopped with me.

I'll end this chapter with one of my biggest flubs in politics. It was an own goal, as they say in soccer, a totally avoidable mistake that was mine and mine alone.

In May of 2021, as the pandemic was easing, we were planning to relax restrictions on gatherings in restaurants and bars. But just before that happened, I went out with a few friends to a fun dive bar in East Lansing, the Landshark. We gathered in the basement, and at first, we were sitting at several tables in compliance with the existing rules: no more than six people at a table, and tables had to be at least six feet apart.

Since there was no one else in the restaurant, someone said, "Let's push these tables together." Maybe they thought that even though we were more than six people, we were one party, so it was okay. But I knew better, and I should have said no. I don't know where my head was that day, because no sooner were we all at one table than someone else said, "Let's get a picture!" If I'd been trying to hide what we were doing, I would have stood up, or said no. Instead, I smiled along with my friends, and after someone snapped the photo, she posted it to Facebook.

Not surprisingly, this caused a minor uproar. As well it should have! I knew I'd screwed up, so the next day I made a statement. "Yesterday, I went with friends to a local restaurant," I said. "As more people arrived, the tables were pushed together. Because we were all vaccinated, we didn't stop to think about it. In retrospect, I should have thought about it. I am human. I made a mistake, and I apologize."

We are all human. And we all fall short sometimes. But that doesn't need to be the end of the story.

TELL PEOPLE YOU CARE ABOUT THEM

After our mom and dad split up, Liz, Richard, and I lived the way so many kids of divorce do, shuttling back and forth between our parents' houses. It's hard to live in two places, and there's always an adjustment period when you go from one to the other. As the oldest child, I was always worrying about how my younger siblings were dealing with all of this. But at some point, I also began worrying a little bit about my dad.

Whenever he'd drop us off at Mom's, he always seemed so sad. I knew he was going back to an empty house, and he didn't try to hide the fact that he missed us when we weren't around.

I began hiding little notes in his house—many of them written on those notepads he gave me for Christmas—so he'd find them after he got home. I'd put them under his pillow, or in his briefcase. They were mostly short little messages, just a way of letting him know I was thinking about him, because I couldn't bear the idea of him feeling so sad without us around. Years later, Dad told me how much those little notes meant to him. He actually saved a lot of them—including one that he framed and hung in his bathroom, where it still hangs to this day.

It's easy to let people know you're thinking about them. My daughters still remember that when they were about to go to sleepaway camp, I drew little smiley faces on their stomachs in permanent marker, so that whenever they changed into pajamas, they'd have a reminder that I was thinking about them. Years later, the three of us got little tattoos—the same design, but slightly different for each of us—that serve the same purpose.

So don't be afraid to show people that you care. Not long ago, a mom and her young daughter saw me on the plane they were boarding, and they decided to write me notes, then ask a flight attendant to deliver them. When I read these two sweet notes thanking me for my work as governor, it absolutely made my day—especially the one from the daughter. Showing someone you care is so powerful, even a ten-year-old can lift a governor's spirits with a kind word.

As a parent, I can tell you, the most treasured notes I get are the handwritten notes from my kids. I keep every one of them. And remember, a note that might take you twenty seconds to write can give someone a lifetime of good feeling—and a nice piece of art for the bathroom.

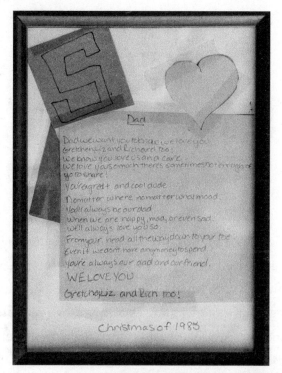

Richard, Liz, me, and our dad at Short's Brewery in Elk Rapids

CHAPTER 10

BE A HAPPY WARRIOR

In 2018, when I ran for governor for the first time, a political action committee called Emily's List offered to send a debate coach to work with me. I'd done a lot of debates during my campaigns for the State House and Senate, but you can always learn something new, and I was excited to get tips from a pro.

Because Emily's List focuses on getting women candidates elected, it felt a bit ironic that they sent over a male coach. But our session started out well. He told me that the Happy Warrior always wins the debate—meaning, whoever looks like they're having the most fun is the person viewers see as the winner, no matter what was actually said.

So far, so good! But then he gave me a piece of advice about how to project that. In a debate where the candidates are standing at podiums, you usually get a blank piece of paper and a pen. "As soon as you get to the podium," he said, "draw a smiley face at the top of your paper to remind yourself to smile."

Like every woman in the history of the world, having a man tell me to smile actually has the opposite effect. More important, I knew it wouldn't work, unless the goal was to remind myself to roll my eyes. There was a zero percent chance that I was going to take this advice, and while the coach went on to give me some very good pointers after that, I couldn't stop thinking about that stupid smiley face.

A few days later, Marc and I went to Detroit to see Kevin Hart do a show on his "Irresponsible" tour. One of the openers was a comedian named Na'im Lynn, and he had a line that made me laugh so hard my drink almost came out of my nose.

It was a joke about how, back in the day, women didn't say outright when they were having their period. If a guy wanted to go out with his girlfriend at the wrong time of the month, she'd say, "You can't. Because my friend's in town." This was so true—when I was in high school, girls who were having their period used to say, "My aunt Flo is visiting!" But now, Na'im went on, women own what is happening. Now, if he asks to come over at his girlfriend's time of the month, she says, "You can't. Because it's Shark Week, motherfucker!"

That line cracked me up, and it also seemed like a sign of empowerment, that young women today didn't feel embarrassed about having their periods. So when the next gubernatorial debate rolled around four days later, I decided to use it. I had a little shark painted on one of my fingernails. And when I walked to the podium, I wrote "SW, MF" at the top of my paper—because I knew that, much more than any smiley face, would bring out my Happy Warrior.

In fact, it put me in such a good mood, I decided to have a little fun at the sound check. My opponent, Michigan attorney general Bill Schuette, was a textbook Republican candidate— very conservative, very buttoned-up. When the audio techs asked us to test our mics at the beginning of the debate, he leaned into his and said, "This is Bill Schuette on duty for the people of Michigan!" Silence. Then it was my turn.

"My name is Gretchen Whitmer," I said. "Welcome to Shark Week!" Everyone on my side of the room busted out laughing. My people knew why I'd said it, because I'd been telling everyone about the joke, but Bill's people looked at me like, *She's lost her mind.* It seemed to knock him a little off balance. I was feeling loose and funny, and I think I won that debate before it even started.

From that moment on, every time I've given a big speech or participated in a debate, I write "SW, MF" at the top of the page. It always helps relax me—though there was one moment in 2020 when I might have gotten a bit too relaxed.

The Democratic National Convention was scheduled to be held in Wisconsin that year, but because of the pandemic, it was mostly virtual. I had been asked to give a speech at ten p.m. on one of the nights, and we decided I would deliver it from a small room in a union hall, the UAW Local 652 in Lansing. The convention dates had been pushed, so this was happening in mid-August, when Michigan is at its hottest, and the temperature inside that room was toasty.

My speech would be carried live, so I was a little nervous, and the stifling atmosphere (and hot TV lights) didn't help. Everyone was masked except for me, and the vibe in the room just felt off. As we waited for the signal to go live, I said, "It's too tense in here! Somebody say something funny!" At which point my deputy chief of staff, Zack Pohl, said, "Remember, Governor, it's Shark Week!"

I smiled and said, "It's not just Shark Week. It's Shark Week"— and then I mouthed the word "motherfucker." Everyone laughed. I looked back at the cameras, and when a few more seconds went by without going live, I looked at Zack again, wagged my finger and said, "I have learned about the hot mic." I absolutely knew better than to say the word out loud with microphones all around. What I didn't expect was that someone would leak the video, showing me very clearly mouthing it.

Seconds later, the feed went live, and I gave my speech. "Hello, America!" I began. "I'm Governor Gretchen Whitmer. Or as Donald Trump calls me, 'that woman from Michigan.'" I spoke for about four minutes, talking about how the Obama-Biden administration had saved the auto industry, praising the workers who kept our economy going during the pandemic, and ending with an acknowledgment of the more than 160,000 people who'd lost their lives to Covid. "Generation after generation, our nation has been defined by what we do. Or what we fail to do," I concluded. "In the memory of all those we've lost, let us act. Let us heal as one nation. Let us find the strength to do the work."

It was a strong speech, and I was honored to have been asked to deliver it. When the camera lights clicked off, I was relieved at how well it had gone. I went to sleep feeling good that night—a feeling that lasted right up to the moment the following morning when my staff told me my Shark Week comment was going viral.

Of the many things I'd said that night, this was the one people were going to remember. I was embarrassed that I'd blown my big opportunity to deliver a message that mattered. What a stupid mistake! I should have known better. My lieutenant governor, Garlin Gilchrist, gave me an opportunity to acknowledge the moment, tweeting "What week is it, @gretchenwhitmer?" I replied with a Discovery Channel GIF of a shark gliding through the water. But I was just beside myself.

As the day went on, though, it started to seem like people saw the gaffe as more hilarious than horrifying. My staff said, "Let's lean into it," and so we did. I explained the whole backstory—the debate coach, the comedy show, and the use of the phrase as a motivator—on a BuzzFeed News podcast. "It's funny," I said. "And it's about women's empowerment, and it makes me smile."

Embracing this moment of levity (and foul language) was the right move, turning an embarrassing moment into an empowering one. The head of Discovery Channel sent me a boxful of official Shark Week gear, and someone else started making and sending me shark pillows. As with "That Woman from Michigan," "It's Shark Week, motherfuckers" merch popped up on Etsy and elsewhere, with people selling candles, T-shirts, and even Covid masks with the quote. I got shark pins made and handed them out to staffers, Marc bought me a ceramic shark dish, and Liz baked me a beautiful birthday cake that read "It's Shark Cake, MF."

I even got a shark tattoo, which I've never revealed in public—even though it is, let's be honest, way cooler than any smiley-face tattoo could ever be.

• • • •

The best way—and really, the only way—to be a Happy Warrior is to embrace who you are, no matter what others might think or say. We all have our quirks and special traits, and accepting them in yourself will make your path through the world smoother.

I could have tried to hide the fact that I'm a klutz, but that would only make things worse when I inevitably trip on a microphone cord or fall out of a car. Once, at a fundraiser, I was supposed to deliver some remarks while standing on a staircase. The host said, "Don't trip!" I said, "I won't!" and then I sure enough did and went sprawling. I popped up like a jack-in-the-box, laughing and shouting, "I'm fine!" because what else could I do?

All the Whitmers have a tendency to be extremely goofy. We could fight it, but what would be the point? That weirdness is gonna poke its way out in some form or another, so we might as well embrace it.

We also have a tendency to bring it out in each other. One day, Liz and I were talking about the discussion around women's body types. Why are we always compared to fruits? Like, *She's pear-shaped*, or *She's an apple*. Liz and I share clothes sometimes, and we've noticed that I need larger pants and smaller tops, and she needs the reverse. So, as we were having this discussion, we decided that I'm a T. rex and she's a Minotaur. It's silly, but we laughed hysterically, imagining me with little useless T. rex arms and her as a buff half monster.

Liz's alternate cover design for this book.

While my kids acknowledge that Liz and Richard are weird, they say I'm the weirdest of the three. But there's a good reason for that. My siblings are at a steady level of weird all the time. I'm the governor, so I have to behave (relatively) normally during my work life. But when I get home, I set the weirdness free. My nieces and nephews tend to see me as two different people. They'll see me on TV and think, *Oh, there's my aunt, the governor.* And then there's Aunt Gretchen the weirdo, who owns a cardboard cutout of herself from a campaign event and likes to hide it in closets and scare the crap out of visitors.

Richard, Liz, and I had great role models in learning how to embrace our quirks: our parents.

Dad was a serious, suit-wearing guy at work, but with us, he was a total goofball. He loved to sing "O Sole Mio" at top volume in restaurants, which made us want to hide under the table. He'd wear silver moon boots to our high school basketball games, just to embarrass us. When our friends came over, he'd give them a dribble glass, then watch deadpan as they tried to figure out why lemonade was dripping down their faces. And he called us special names—I was Nehcterg Rehtse Remtihw, Liz was Htebazile and Richard was Drahcir. Yep, our names backward. His middle name is Elliott—Ttoille (pronounced "Toiley"), which cracked us up. He's well named, as he loves to Kcid around.

Mom just knew who she was and embraced it. Although she was a high-powered attorney, she loved the color pink—everything from vibrant fuchsia to bright, candy-colored Barbie pink. Her signature lipstick color was Revlon Softsilver Red, which, despite its name, is most definitely pink. One of her favorite jackets was fuchsia, and one day as she left her office to go to court, a colleague who was also a close friend said to her, "Sherry! You can't go to court wearing pink!" Maybe she thought my mother would look too girly or soft in such a traditionally feminine color. But Mom just looked at her and said, "What are you talking about? Fuchsia is my power color." If anyone in the courtroom didn't like it, well, that was their problem, not hers.

I love fuchsia too. It's an energetic, happy color, and I feel good when I'm wearing it. It's a tie to my mom—and to my grandmother Nino, who used to plant those pink flowers in the park across the street from her house. What greater power can you have than carrying your mother and grandmother with you in the clothes you're wearing?

Though I tend to put on a leather jacket in the moments when I need real armor, I've worn fuchsia for some of the most meaningful moments in my political life. I wore it when I signed the legislation overturning the "rape insurance" (which I signed into law using pink ink). I wore it when I debated my 2022 opponent in the governor's race. And I wore it when I delivered my inaugural address in 2023—a year in which women were reelected to all three of the top statewide offices in Michigan. So, pink is my power color too.

For me, being a Happy Warrior means embracing your true self and looking for the lighter side in any situation. My two terms as governor haven't been easy. We've faced once-in-a-lifetime catastrophes, pandemics and floods and polar vortexes, as well as protests and threats. It would have been easy to feel crushed by the weight of these events, or bitter that they all happened while I was in the governor's office. But that would have been unfair to the people of Michigan, and a luxury none of us could afford. So I just keep pushing forward, looking for solutions, listening and learning, and using humor to defuse difficult moments whenever I can.

A couple of summers ago, I had a conversation with my mother's sister, my aunt Betsy. This was during one of the difficult periods in my first term, and I was particularly missing my mom that day.

"Betsy, if Mom were here, what would she say to me?" I asked.

She thought for a moment, then replied, "I don't know what she would say to you, Gretchen. But you're so much like her, because even in the worst circumstances, your mother could find something funny. And you're exactly the same way." I can't tell you how much it meant to me to hear that.

Whenever I'm feeling low, I think about those words. I carry my mother with me, in memory and in our shared view of the world. I carry my father, too, in his commitment to doing what's right and his love of family. I hope to shine a light for my daughters in the same way my parents did for me. And in the process, I hope to do right by the people of my state, who have entrusted me with the greatest honor imaginable in making me their governor.

EPILOGUE

I started this book by telling you about my grandmother Nino. Now I'll end it with a story about her husband—my grandfather, our beloved Dano.

Dana Whitmer was the superintendent of schools in Pontiac, a city of 85,000 people just north of Detroit that became a flashpoint in the fight over racial integration. In May of 1971, the US Court of Appeals ruled that Pontiac had to pursue busing, to better integrate the city's mostly white school system. White anti-busing residents created the National Action Group (NAG) to organize protests. And when the school year began, some mothers actually chained themselves to buses in an effort to stop integration.

The National Action Group was vocal and disruptive, but when the Ku Klux Klan showed up, the situation turned violent. On August 30—one week after I was born—the Klan blew up ten empty school buses, shocking not only Pontiac, but the whole country.

"There is fear," my grandfather told a reporter at *Time* magazine. Many Black families didn't want their kids to be bused to unfamiliar neighborhoods and schools, and many white residents didn't want Black students studying with their children. My grandfather was caught in the middle, trying to navigate a situation where everyone was unhappy while knowing he had a job to do—to keep the community safe and educate children. Nothing was going to stop him from delivering on both.

Dano was unflappable through all of it. They used to call him the Silver Fox, because he had a shock of white hair and a piercing, confident gaze. Throughout August and September of 1971, he worked long hours to keep the peace in Pontiac while upholding the law. Occasionally during this period, the phone would ring at night at my grandparents' house. Nino would answer, and someone on the other end would say, "Your husband's dead. We killed him." Or: "Your husband better watch his back. We're coming for him." She never knew who the callers were, or whether they were telling the truth. And sometimes, like on the day the Klan blew up the buses, she couldn't reach him to make sure he was okay. It was a brutal time for my grandmother.

For generations, the Whitmer family has valued and pursued public service. As a rule, we believe that all people are equal, and that the government must help ensure that we all have access to the opportunity to live our version of the American dream. We're willing to fight for those values, even in the face of threats. When the apparent assassination plot against me came to light, I initially didn't make the connection between what had happened to Dano and what was happening to me. But when my dad pointed it out, I felt proud to be part of that family history, and even more determined to stand up against domestic terrorists.

A while back, a therapist asked me, "Is there anything you would die for?" My instant response was, "My daughters." As the last few years have unfolded, I've thought a lot about that question. And the truth is, there are many other things worth giving one's life for. Fighting for justice, for the right of people to live in dignity and peace, and for our freedom to control what happens to our own bodies.

As governor of Michigan, I'm fortunate to be in a position to fight for those things. Our response to Covid wasn't perfect, but I believe that the steps we took saved lives. I believe that our efforts to protect women's bodily autonomy have made a difference. So much is counting on the work my team and I have been doing, and I'm proud of that. While the threats that have come with it are shocking and disturbing, I discovered that I can deal with almost anything. And I've learned what really matters: that while I'm individually not that important, the work that I do is. What we're doing matters, and there's no place I'd rather be than right here, right now.

I've always loved the famous "Man in the Arena" quote from a speech Theodore Roosevelt once gave. In every campaign, and during every term I serve, I share it with my team to remind them that while our work can be heavy and hard, it takes guts to do what we're doing:

> It is not the critic who counts; not the man who points out how the strong man stumbles, or where the doer of deeds could have done them better. The credit belongs to the man who is actually in the arena, whose face is marred by dust and sweat and blood; who strives valiantly; who errs, who comes short again and again, because there is no effort without error and shortcoming; but who does actually strive to do the deeds; who knows the great enthusiasms, the great devotions; who spends himself in a worthy cause; who at the best knows in the end the triumph of high achievement, and who at the worst, if he fails, at least fails while daring greatly, so that his place shall never be with those cold and timid souls who neither know victory nor defeat.

Though these words were written more than a hundred years ago, they're just as true today—except for two things. The "man" may be a woman. And she may just be wearing fuchsia.

Showing off my "Michigan mittens." I love my state.

ACKNOWLEDGMENTS

Thank you to . . .

Liz Whitmer Gereghty, my sister, best friend, chief bridal offi-cer, anger translator, and project manager in this undertaking. I couldn't have done this without you.

Lisa Dickey, who melded so well into Whitmer world, we gave her honorary "Half-Whit" status. With her guidance and skill, we wrote the book we wanted in record time. I couldn't have hoped for a better partnership.

All successes are team efforts, and I have the best damn team in the nation.

My official team: everyone in the executive office of the governor and my cabinet, I could never have navigated these years without you. My campaign crews: thank you for helping me put my best self out there for the people of Michigan. My lawyers (and friends): thanks for keeping me out of trouble.

True Gretch team: Simon & Schuster, in particular Mindy Marques, Priscilla Painton, Jon Karp, Hana Park, and Mark LaFlaur, Julia McCarthy, Alex Kelleher, Michael McCartney, Jeannie Ng, Elizabeth Blake-Linn, Jenica Nasworthy, Jessie

Bowman, and Anum Shafqat, thank you for helping to make this book a reality. To Jay Mandel and everyone at WME, thank you for your support.

I am grateful to all the incredible people who have loved, encouraged, taught, befriended, supported, and challenged me—and that goes double for my family:

My husband, Marc, whose unwavering support and boundless enthusiasm still keep me on my toes.

My dad and mom, for setting an example of how to serve, to focus on what's important, and to laugh when things go off the rails.

Brother Richard, an amazing person, brother, and friend—who's always been "the grease" that makes everything run smoother.

Kevin and Doug, the best dogs on the planet.

My daughters, Sherry and Sydney: you ground me, amuse me, and have taught me many things. Thank you for bringing so much light and love into my life. This book is for you.

Q&A WITH GRETCHEN'S DAUGHTERS, SHERRY AND SYDNEY, WITH QUESTIONS ASKED BY THEIR AUNT LIZ (AND OCCASIONAL INTERJECTIONS FROM GRETCHEN)

With my daughters, Sherry (left) and Sydney.
Campaigning involves the whole family.

Does it feel strange to have a mother who is also a governor?
Sherry: If your parent is working, most of the time you don't really know what they're doing. Generally, you're just kind of like, "Well, my mom works in healthcare" or "Oh, my dad works in finance. . . ." You're not with them all the time. But

with a parent who is often in the media, so directly involved in so many people's lives . . . The things that they're doing are put in your face more often than a lot of other parents' jobs.

Sydney: If I'm at school, I'm not really thinking about what Mom is doing, but then I go on my phone and I see that *The Michigan Daily* has just posted an article and all of a sudden, her face has popped up on my screen and I'm like, *Oh, hi.* But it's also weird in the respect that I kind of separate "Mom" from "governor." Because when I see her on TV, I think, *Oh, that's just what she does.* That's the governor and she's being interviewed. But if she's at home, she's just Mom.

How do you feel when you are in public together and eighty-seven different people want selfies? Does that feel weird?
Sherry: Personally, I don't *love* when we're sitting down at a restaurant and someone comes up to us, even for a brief period. It changes our experience from a family event to something different. But I think people connect with Mom on such a personal level that it feels like it's okay. And I am grateful that she's doing work that people think is good and important and that they want to show their support in public and on social media. Largely, I think people are respectful and I understand the urge.

Sydney: Yeah, I agree with that. To Sherry's point, I think it's awesome that people love her so much, but again, she's so busy,

160

so when we're getting a meal or something, I only have so much time with her.

The first term was challenging on many levels and kind of unprecedented. What did you think when your mom decided to run for a second term?

Sydney: Honestly, I supported it 100 percent, because even though the first term was pretty rough, she also did a lot of good. And I feel like a lot of those efforts would've been left unfinished if she hadn't run for a second term. I think that's more important.

Sherry: Yeah, I've thought about this recently—it was rough because people did come to our house with guns to look threatening. There was a lot of attention. And I wouldn't want to experience that again. But I think sacrificing some privacy, some family time for Mom to do good and important work is worth it. I think she's a great governor, and I am glad she ran for a second term.

What is the most important thing your mother has taught you?

Sydney: Treat everyone with grace and respect and kindness. I have had conflicts in friendships and relationships, and when venting to my mom, she always reminds me to try to see their perspective—that it's not all about me, and there are all kinds of context and experiences that I might not know about.

Sherry: I do think it is a trait of the entire family, to respond with humor. That's something that I've really incorporated into how I am as a person. Making something humorous can shine some light on a very heavy situation. Humor can make people feel lighter, quicker, and that can be a superpower or tool to use in situations where it can get pretty dark.

Does your mother ever embarrass you in public?
Sherry (to Gretchen): I don't think you ever embarrassed me in public.

Gretchen: Sometimes I'll call you out and say, "Clap, children!"

Sherry: In public, I assume the role of representing you, and especially in settings like a fundraiser, I understand that you're going to be calling me out. I don't think you've embarrassed me in public, but in private? Damn right! Something that I don't think comes across in your book enough is just how goofy you can be.

Gretchen: We have a whole section on that.

Sherry: Yeah, but people don't really know that you make silly noises, or like . . . It's hard to describe, but in private you are more of a carefree, ha-ha-ha-let's-do-something-funny-and-laugh-about-it kind of a person. You're not very serious in private.

Sherry and Sydney make fun of me as I hold up
Papi the papier-mâché dog.

Sydney: All the "embarrassing" things that you do aren't actually embarrassing—I think they're funny. Sometimes I'll roll my eyes for comedic effect and pretend that I'm embarrassed, but I'm not. I'm in on the joke.

Gretchen: I've got to work harder at that. I used to embarrass you when I dropped you off at school.

Sherry: You'd roll down the window and go, "No fighting and no biting!"

Gretchen: And I would take my teeth out. Remember when we were driving to school and there was an East Lansing school bus in front of us and all the kids were looking back at us. . . . Do you remember that?

Sherry: I don't remember. I think that's a coping mechanism.

Did you take any shit from your peers when the schools closed, and prom and graduation were canceled?
Sherry: No, because I think people understood—at least my group of friends—that it was necessary. I think Sydney might be a better person to ask because it happened so late in my high school career that the only things left were spring break, prom, and graduation. And those were things where I thought, *Okay, I've had the rest of senior year, and it does suck, but it isn't the end of the world to miss out on.* I do remember crying about it, but at the same time, I think the things I lost out on were necessary for the safety of others. And my class at least accepted that and moved on. There was a new chapter waiting ahead, so that was kind of exciting.

The only thing that I remember getting a little bit of shit for in high school was when Mom tried to ban flavored vapes. I remember a lot of kids in my grade posting on Snapchat being like, "The governor thinks she's going to take away my vape." And I'm like, *Oh my God.*

Gretchen: You told me that, and I mentioned it in an interview, remember? And you got so pissed.

Sherry: Oh, I think I did. I thought, *Don't let people know that I know that they're talking crap about you!*

Sydney: I personally didn't get a ton of shit thrown my way directly, but I would hear from my friends that people were talking bad about Mom, and that would kind of get to me. But then I also didn't really care, because the people that were talking about her, I thought, *whatever.* I also feel like I flew under the radar, so people didn't really care as much, I guess.

Sherry: Yeah, that's the thing with high schoolers: either you kind of know what's going on but you don't really care about the government, or that's your whole thing. I think the transition to college is when people really start to get into politics, because you can vote, so people understand that it is a civic obligation, and you pay more attention.

Have you learned anything from your mom about dealing with bullies?
Sherry: Knowing that you can remove yourself from a situation is powerful. When a situation is hurtful or seems to be toxic for both parties involved or someone is attempting to bully you, it helps to recognize that you don't need to engage, and, if it's better for you, you can take a step back. And if you don't have the opportunity to do that, then recognizing that asking for help isn't a weakness— it's something that is very necessary in some situations.

Sydney: I totally agree. I was once friends with someone whose other friends didn't like me. And instead of fighting and giving them my energy, I realized that it's just not worth it. As long as I can remove myself from the situation, I'll be fine. And that's what I did, and I'm so happy that I made that choice.

Doug and Kevin as sunflowers

Why did you name your dogs Kevin and Doug?
Sydney: We originally wanted a person name, and Kevin comes from the TV show *The Office*—Kevin Malone. We think he's so funny. And we are also huge fans of *21 Jump Street* with Jonah Hill and Channing Tatum. We decided to name Doug after Jonah Hill's undercover persona, Doug McQuaid.

Going back to the first term and having protesters outside your house, how did you feel about it? Were you scared? How did you cope with it?

Sydney: For me, I woke up on a random morning, hearing air horns and super loud music playing, and I was like, *What is going on?* And then I look out the window and I see that huge Trump float and a ton of people outside holding guns. My initial reactions were shock and fear. But I realized that we're well protected, and it didn't seem like a situation where I would actually be in danger, if that makes any sense. I felt fine after a while, but there was that initial shock.

Sherry: I didn't feel like I was in danger. I think if someone really wanted to hurt us, it wouldn't be by protesting outside of our house. I don't think protesters are inherently violent, and I think their display of guns was intended to intimidate but not necessarily act.

Sydney: The only times that I felt unsafe are when Mom is on official business surrounded by a bunch of people we don't know and the only people that are looking out for her are four people in suits.

And one of you was with your mom at the Cherry Festival that day?

Sherry: That was me. And that was kind of what I was referencing: being in a big group of people in an open area—that's

167

genuinely what the situation was. The unknown of people's agendas when her presence is public is the scary part.

Since we're talking about guns, what advice would you give to a younger person who is dealing with lockdown drills?
Sydney: In our district, we had counselors at our school. I feel like people are generally getting better at providing resources for that kind of thing. Having someone to talk to is very helpful. I also think technology like your phone helps: when we would have lockdown drills or actual shooting lockdowns, I could text my mom or make sure that my sister, who's in another classroom on the other side of school, is okay.

Sherry: Sadly, I think it's something that is now a part of how children grow up. And until a big change happens or until we hold more people accountable or pass stricter gun laws, drills are what you have to do to at least keep children safe. People our age have grown up more aware of our surroundings. I don't think that's a lesson that will ever be bad, but being so aware of your mortality at a young age is definitely difficult.

Talking to people from a generation that didn't have to live with this can feel like we're not really understanding one another. But talking to other people our age reminds us that we are all in the same boat. Being anxious and angry that we have to live like this can really empower people to make change in my generation, hopefully.

How do you feel about it when your mom just can't stop trending on social media?
Sherry: For real? (Laughter)

Sydney: I just roll my eyes.

Sherry: What's really funny are TikTok comments when Mom is doing something or she posted a video and I go through the comments and people are like, "I love Big Gretch," or "I'm so proud that we have Big Gretch." I love it. I think it's great.

Sydney: I was thinking about this in my poli-sci class earlier this week. I'm like, *What if I just stood up and said, "Yeah, I'm Big Gretch's daughter"?* People would be like, what?

What's the cringiest thing your mother has ever done?
Sydney: This was already mentioned: she would roll the window down when dropping us off at school and yell, "No fighting, no biting."

Sherry: I don't know. She hasn't really done anything cringey to the point where I'm like, *Oh my God, I can't believe you just did that.*

Well, Gretchen, you have some work to do.
Gretchen: Challenge accepted!

If you could wave a wand and change one thing about politics right now, what would it be?
Sydney: I would make things less volatile and divided. I think that's my biggest thing.

Sherry: Oh, no. If I had a magic wand, I'd make it so that every time someone spread misinformation or told a lie, an alarm would sound.

How do you feel about sharks? Do you share your mother's affinity?
Sherry: I'm terrified of sharks. I have tried to love them as an animal, I truly have, but they scare the hell out of me. Any creature in open water that can graze past my leg? No, I don't want it. It could be a fish, it could be a snake, it could be a whale—nope, nope, nope.

Sydney: But sharks don't want to harm you. They're only protecting themselves.

Okay, so those are our opinions on sharks. But the whole Shark Week thing, how do you view that?
Sydney: I think it's great because that was kind of a slipup on Mom's part. And as she says in the book, she totally regretted doing it. But then, over the next week, she kind of started owning it, and people got on board, and it was hilarious. I think owning your mistakes is pretty powerful.

Sherry: I think it's awesome because not only is it an analogy for badass women, but she also swore. The whole package of it is pretty badass. So I'm on board and I like it.

Okay. Lightning round. First one that just came out of this conversation: Do you read the comments?
Sydney: Yes.

Sherry: Only occasionally.

Is a hot dog a sandwich?
Sydney: No. No.

Sherry: It's not a sandwich. It's not.

Have you ever parted your hair in the middle?
Sherry: Yes.

Did anything bad happen to you when you did that?
Sherry: No.

What do you think about your mom's True Gretch playlist?
Sydney: I think it's good.

Sherry: I have some tweaks.

Okay. What would you add?

Sherry: A K-pop song. It's not internationally comprehensive. That's my answer.

Sydney: Greta Van Fleet. Something by them.

What would be your number one desert island book?

Sydney: I know you probably want us to say *True Gretch*, but that's not the case. . . . I choose *The Selection*. It's a really corny YA book, but it's so good.

TikTok, Instagram, Facebook, Snapchat, X/Twitter, or none of the above?

Sydney: TikTok.

Sherry: Twitter. I do use TikTok a lot, but Twitter is my general newsletter for all of my special interests.

Have you ever written an actual letter, on paper?

Sherry: Yes. Yes. We write 'em every time it's someone's birthday. Well, Mom's birthday or Dad's birthday.

Speaking of dads, tell me your best dad joke.

Sherry: I saw this question, and I didn't have one prepared.

Sydney: What's red and bad for your teeth? A brick.

RESOURCES

It's always okay to ask for help. Below are resources (mostly US-based) that I think might be helpful for you or a friend who may be struggling. The websites of most of these organizations have information on how to support those who may need help, or how to advocate for yourself if you don't have the support you need at home. A good first step is to seek out a trusted adult: a parent or other relative, a teacher, a counselor, or someone who can help you access what you need. You deserve it.

988 Lifeline Suicide Prevention
A 24/7 hotline
Call: 988
Text: 988
Chat or ASL: 988lifeline.org

211
Find local mental health and crisis resources
Call: 211

Crisis Text Line
Help with gun violence, anxiety, eating disorders, depression, suicide, self-harm (24/7 hotline)
Text: "HOME" to 741741
Chat: crisistextline.org

National Alliance on Mental Illness
Call: 1 (800) 950-6264
Text: "helpline" to 62640
Visit: NAMI.org

RAINN / National Sexual Assault Hotline
Rape, Abuse & Incest National Network (24/7 hotline)
Call: 1 (800) 656-4673
Chat: online.rainn.org

The Trevor Project
LGBTQ+ resources (24/7 hotline)
Text: "START" to 678-678
Call: 1 (866) 488-7386
Chat: thetrevorproject.org

National Domestic Violence Hotline
A 24/7 hotline
Text: "START" to 88788
Call: 1 (800) 799-7233
Chat: the hotline.org

National Human Trafficking Hotline
A 24/7 hotline
Call: 1 (888) 373-7888
TTY: 711
Text: 233733
Chat: humantraffickinghotline.org/chat

National Center for Missing and Exploited Children
A 24/7 hotline
Call: 1 (800) 843-5678
Visit: missingkids.org

Substance Abuse & Mental Health Services Administration
A 24/7 hotline
Call: 1 (800) 662-4357
TTY: 1 (800) 487-4889
Text: your zip code to 435748 (to find services near you)

National Council on Problem Gambling
A 24/7 hotline
Call: 1 (800) 426-2537
Text: 800GAM
Chat: ncpgambling.org/help-treatment/chat/

PHOTO CREDITS

p. 6: Family photos

p. 14: Gary Shrewsbury Photography

p. 15: Liz Gereghty

p. 23: Family photo

p. 46: Gary Shrewsbury Photography

p. 54: Gary Shrewsbury Photography

p. 66: Photo by Julia Pickett / Michigan Governor's Office

p. 75: Family photo

p. 82: Family photo

p. 96: Gretchen Whitmer

p. 109: Gary Shrewsbury Photography

p. 110: Gary Shrewsbury Photography

p. 127: Gary Shrewsbury Photography

p. 139 *(top)*: Gary Shrewsbury Photography

p. 139 *(bottom)*: Family photo

p. 145: Family photo

p. 147: Liz Gereghty

p. 155: Gary Shrewsbury Photography

p. 159: Family photo

p. 163: Family photo

p. 166: Family photo

ABOUT THE AUTHORS

Gretchen Whitmer is the governor of Michigan and a rising figure in American politics. Known for her bold and plainspoken style, Whitmer is a national voice on the rights of women, voters, and the LGBTQ+ community. She rose to national prominence for her leadership in 2020 during the Covid-19 pandemic, when her efforts to save lives in the state prompted the former president to call her "that woman from Michigan." Later that year, she was the target of a domestic terror plot that was foiled by the FBI and state police. Whitmer is a lifelong Michigander who first ran for office at age twenty-nine, has served in both state houses and as a prosecutor, and has never lost an election. She is the proud mother of two daughters, a huge Detroit Lions fan, and the subject of the song "Big Gretch" by rapper Gmac Cash.

A longtime book collaborator, **Lisa Dickey** has helped clients write more than twenty nonfiction books, including twelve *New York Times* bestsellers. For more information, visit lisadickey.com.